TAKE IT TO THE NEXT LEVEL

PERFORMANCE PRINCIPLES FOR LIFE

Take It... TO THE NEXT LEVEL

Doug Reese

ISBN 1-929478-63-1

Cross Training Publishing
317 West Second Street
Grand Island, NE 68801
(308) 384-5762

This book is manufactured in the United States of America.
Library of Congress Cataloging in Publication Data in Progress.

Dedication

This book is dedicated to my family: to Matt, Chris, Reilly, and especially my wife, Rosanne, who has given up so much, and sacrificed so greatly in support of my coaching, recruiting, and travels over the many seasons of competition. You all have provided for me untold joy and inspiration. I love you guys!

acknowledgements

In the summer of 2000, Chad Curtis, then of the Texas Rangers penned a weekly column in the Religion section of the *Arlington News.* Chad wrote about the challenge of being a professional athlete while trying to "do what Jesus would do."

Chad's columns challenged me not only to look at sport from a Biblical perspective, but to coach it from the Master's Playbook, Chad's influence led me to begin writing this selection of devotionals from not only the sports news, but from the pages of my life in the game.

This book would not be possible with the love and passion I have for sport. Sport is more than just a game, it is a microcosm of life itself. It has been my greatest classroom, and my greatest teacher.

Setting out as a young athlete, then as a rookie coach, I wanted to leave my mark on the game, but instead I have found that rather leaving my signature on sport that coaches, teammates, and sport left their mark on me.

This book would have not be possible without the support and encouragement of my teammate in sport, life, and in Christ; Ted Toburen. Although there have been so many coaches and teammates over the years I owe much to, there is neither time nor space to adequately acknowledge all of you. Anyone who has stepped on the field of battle with me that possessed focus, intensity, and heart, I say "THANK YOU!" You are my heroes!

Take It to the Next Level

I have been blessed to have been involved with sport since my earliest memories. I have been fascinated from the start with the beauty, the skill, the desire, and the discipline it takes to perform at a high level. As a child, I listened intently to stories my grandfather told of the great athletes of his day. His tales, energy, and passion for sport pumped into my veins the same love and desire flowing through his.

I learned long ago that sport cuts across all languages, political and geographic boundaries, and cultures. Sport is a microcosm of life. It is one of the best teachers I know. What I learned on the ball fields, from the demanding practice sessions, and then in competition was more than technique and tactics, more than winning and losing—I learned about life itself.

My life in sport as an athlete, and now as a collegiate and U.S. national coach, has been a quest to reach the next level. Along the way I learned a lot of lessons; how to sacrifice, to be disciplined, and to pay the price that victory requires. Sport, my teammates and my many coaches, have been great mentors. This was the inspiration for the web-based sport ministry, "To The Next Level" (www.tothenextlevel.org), to be a coach—a mentor in helping other athletes and coaches from around the world reach the next level in their sport, as well as in their life performance.

This collection of thoughts and writings bring two of my passions together; the love of the LORD Jesus Christ, and the love of sport. Sport was the vehicle that always got my attention; now it is used here to teach Biblical truth—living truth for athletes, coaches, and fans.

Bob Cousy, the great ball-handling guard of the Boston Celtics once said, "Sports create a bond between contemporaries that lasts a lifetime. It also gives your life structure, discipline, and a genuine, sincere, pure fulfillment that few other areas of endeavor provide." The only other thing in the world that surpasses what Cousy describes is a personal relationship with Jesus Christ. It is my hope that this book will light a fire of passion in your heart much like my grandfather did for me many years ago.

Contents

PERFORMANCE PRINCIPLE 1

NEVER LET GO!

Webster defines struggle as "to contend resolutely with an adversary or adverse conditions...to contend resolutely with a task or problem...to advance with violent effort..." In both life and sport a potential struggle can be lurking around the next corner. Consider this story from the Olympic Games:

The longest wrestling bout in Olympic history took place in the semifinals of the Greco-Roman 165 pound division in the 1912 Stockholm Games.

Martin Klein of Estonia competing for Czarist Russia, and Alfred Asikainen of Finland struggled on and on for eleven hours under the hot sun. Every half hour they stopped for a refreshment break before the bout resumed. The pushing, the pummeling, the digging, and the head snaps took a toll on both of them. Finally, Klein pinned Asikainen. However, Klein was so exhausted from the ordeal that he was unable to wrestle in the finals. Claues Johanson of Sweden was given the gold medal by default!

Have you ever wrestled day after day with inner conflicts, feeling as if the bout would never end? Have you known such sorrow that you felt sure God had forgotten you—that He didn't seem to care? Have you endured loss after loss, while it seemed that the enemy had no mercy?

It happens to all of us.

Jacob had not seen his brother Esau in twenty years. Esau was ready to kill him for stealing the family blessing as well as his birthright (Genesis 25:29—27:42). Esau was so angry that he had vowed to kill Jacob as soon as their father, Isaac died (Genesis 27:41).

Jacob was frantic with fear. He collected his thoughts and decided to pray. Jacob cried out, "Save me, I pray, from the hand of my brother Esau….," (Genesis 32:11). Fearing their reunion, Jacob sent a messenger ahead with gifts in hopes of appeasing Esau and gaining his favor.

Then Jacob sent his family and all their possessions across a stream in the other direction, while he stayed behind alone. Then Jacob engaged "a man" and wrestled with him all night long. When the man realized that he could not overpower Jacob, he dislocated Jacob's hip. Then the man said to Jacob, "Let me go, for it is daybreak," (Genesis 32:26).

But Jacob replied, "I will not let you go unless you bless me," (Genesis 32:27).

The man then blessed Jacob, "Your name will no longer be Jacob, but Israel, because you have struggled with God and with men and have overcome," (Genesis 32:28).

Jacob continued wrestling all night long *just to be blessed.* Wrestling with such intensity, for so long is not easy, *it's exhausting!* What we can learn from Jacob is *persistence.*

God encourages persistence in all areas of our lives—not just our athletic pursuits or in our academics, but in every area, including our spiritual lives.

God reminds us that strong character develops as you struggle through the tough situations of life. God doesn't promise us easy challenge matches, but "grind matches" that will test the limits of our faith. In the process God is forming us into champions who can overcome.

Jacob was at the crossroads. He was scared to die at the hand of his own brother. That night on the riverbank Jacob grabbed on to God and wouldn't let go. For the first time in his life he realized that his own strength and wit were not enough. He knew now that his dependence was on God who blesses him. Jacob's relationship with God became essential to his life, and his name was changed to Israel, "he struggles with God."

I encourage you to persevere in your struggles. Go to your knees and pray. Grab on to God and refuse to let go. Keep Him in the center of your life, keep Him in your grasp…and NEVER LET GO!

PERFORMANCE PRINCIPLE 2

GOING ALONG WITH THE CROWD

The NCAA Division I Committee on Infractions has reduced the number of football scholarships, imposed recruiting restrictions, and placed the University of Colorado on probation for two years for violations in the university's football program.

The violations involved impermissible recruiting contacts for a number of years. The committee also found violations involving the provision of clothing to recruits, contacts with athletic representatives, excessive reimbursement of travel expenses for recruits and for improprieties involving recruiting entertainment expenses.

The Infraction Committee in its public report said, "this was a serious case in which a football coaching staff was led by the former head football coach in a calculated attempt to gain a recruiting advantage."

In testimony before the committee, one former football coach said he had "compromised" his integrity by "simply going along with the culture that was out there."

Are we also guilty of compromising our integrity by going along with the crowd? In order to gain a personal advantage, are we willing to view right and wrong through the eyes of those who do not strive to live with integrity?

A popular approach these days says it's okay to take what you want from others as long as you don't get caught. If you are unhappy with your marriage you should get a divorce. Nothing is really right or wrong anymore, so homosexuality, sexual intimacy before marriage, and abortion are acceptable options. The philosophy of our day advises us to do whatever it takes to get what we want, and that what we want is nothing of which to be ashamed. We are no longer bound by the puritanical rules of the past.

But God's laws and precepts never change. "The commandments of the LORD are right, bringing joy to the heart. The commands of the LORD are clear, giving insight to life. Reverence for the LORD is pure, lasting forever. The laws of the LORD are true; each one is fair. They are more desirable than gold, even the finest gold. They are sweeter than honey, even honey dripping from the comb. They are a warning to those who hear them; there is great reward for those who obey them." (Psalm 19:8-11, NLT)

Wisdom is the ancient art, which people have practiced through the ages to skillfully avoid plunging into the pitfalls to which others fall victim. It imparts a disciplined approach to living, and while teaching us to work hard and stay out of mischief, it turns us into leaders others admire.

Wisdom is living a life that honors our parents and coaches, mastering the ability to handle our money and conduct our sexual lives, honoring our employers and our agreements—all of this is the fruit of wisdom. Wisdom is about acquiring self-mastery and an approach towards others that promotes peace.

Wisdom is about implementing proven strategies and tactics in our daily battles. Wisdom is about building character, respect, and honor. Sewn through all this is the very nature of God.

So how do you attain wisdom? How do you avoid being sucked in by the pressure of the world? It starts with fearing God (Proverbs 1:7). The next step is to receive the Word of God as powerful truth and memorize His commands. Then you apply your heart to understand them. It takes work to understand how to implement each command in different situations, but He has promised to help you if you really give it your honest effort. He will provide wisdom to you (Proverbs 2:6). Your job is to seek wisdom diligently and to tightly hold on to it. As you learn to apply wisdom in every situation—no matter what the cost—God's promises will fill your life with blessing.

One of the best ways to seek wisdom is to study the Old Testament book of Proverbs. Read one chapter every day. If today is the fourth day of the month, read the fourth chapter. At the end of one year you will have read the book of Proverbs twelve times—and you will have received a gift of the knowledge of God's very nature and wisdom that far surpasses its value in gold (Proverbs 3:13-14).

Wisdom is power. It is a force that overcomes the lies and deceptions of the world. Plug into that power—the power of the Living God and avoid going along (and down!) with the crowd

PERFORMANCE PRINCIPLE 3

HARDER THAN IT OUGHT TO BE

She has been an Olympic-caliber, middle-distance runner, a world-class heptathlete, and now she is also known as a world-class marathoner after placing second in the 2002 New York Marathon.

Marla Runyan has made a career out of doing the unexpected. In the 2000 Summer Games in Sydney, she was known as the girl who was legally blind because of a degenerative retina condition called Stargardt's disease. She somehow pushed herself to be a straight-A student, a world-class heptathlete, then a Para-Olympian, then an Olympian. In Sydney she finished eighth in the 1,500 meters. In US competition, Runyan holds titles at 3,000 and 5,000 meters. Some say she is the best American runner since Mary Decker Slaney.

To Marla Runyan, almost everything, even the face of someone seated just across the table, is a blur of color and movement and shapes. Because she can't rely on visual help others take for granted, there are tremendous challenges that face her just to run—such as memorizing the course, picking our landmarks, facing street hazards, and just finding the water station.

According to Runyan, she was driven to succeed because of her vision problems. "I can see now how in my high school, my college (years) I had this unyielding drive to accomplish, to achieve, to excel. In many ways, I made life harder than it needed to be, as if it wasn't hard enough."

Marla Runyan isn't alone. Most of us make life much harder than it needs to be. We pile heavy loads upon our own backs, trudging forward, reading our own road maps to success and fulfillment. The load takes a heavy toll on us. The path we take is unforgiving with very few downhill sections. We run a race, in fact, that we cannot win.

We, too, are blind in the race we run. The future is out of focus. We cannot see the next turn, the next bend, or even the finish line.

When we are "crucified with Christ" (Galatians 2:20) and live "united with him in his resurrection" (Romans 6:5), we begin to see more and more of our life's race through the eyes of God. What we thought we saw as critically important begins to fade, and what we once neglected, we now see as beloved by our heavenly Father.

David writes, "Unless the LORD builds the house, its builders labor in vain. Unless the LORD watches over the city, the watchmen stand guard in vain" (Psalm 127:1).

We can no longer build according to our old set of plans, desires, and goals. In fact, when we truly come in submission to the cross, we find we can no longer build anything according to our own design or scheme—nor in our own strength! If we are building on our own, we just make life harder than it ought to be.

Life goes by so fast, and our eternal vision is so limited. We frantically build, yet fail to see that we are building with sand, which will crumble with the swell of the next wave. We struggle to build our athletic careers, our athletic programs, our marriages, our friendships, the list goes on and on. But we are expending great energies and efforts without allowing God to build.

In order for God to properly build, we must first submit to the training program He desires to put us through. He wants to train us into the likeness of His Son, Jesus, learning from His playbook, applying His wisdom and strategies into every part of our life.

We have a choice to run blind, to stumble, to fall, and to make life harder than it ought to be, or we can submit to God's training program, His game plan, and secure peace, contentment and ultimate victory. That only happens when God is allowed to build your life. Turn it over to Him. Surrender it all. Quit making life harder than it ought to be.

PERFORMANCE PRINCIPLE 4

THANKFUL FOR THE GIFT

I was invited to coach at the U.S. Olympic Training Center in Colorado Springs to help prepare our U.S. Women's Freestyle Wrestling Team for the upcoming world championships. I was thrilled and honored to have the opportunity to coach our nation's best athletes at the USOTC.

I always love going to the Olympic Training Center. You feel the spirit of the Olympic movement. You are in an energy-charged, positive environment where countless athletes live and train to reach their goals and Olympic dreams. You catch a vision of what is possible to achieve in this place. I always come away with a fired up attitude.

While I was there the best coaches and athletes this country has to offer were training in preparation for the Men's Freestyle World Championships and the Greco-Roman World Championships. The wrestling room was filled twice a day with the heroes and champions of the sport: Dan Gable, Bobby Douglass, Sergei Beloglazov, Steve Fraser, Kevin Jackson, Rulon Gardener, Tom and Terry Brands, Kendall Cross, Townsend Saunders, Cael Sanderson, Terry Steiner, Chris Bono, and Kenny Monday to mention a few.

To say the least I felt out of place among this crowd. I hadn't won an Olympic medal or a world championship title. I hadn't won a NCAA title or even a high school state championship. There were other coaches who have achieved more, who deserved to be here more than I. They either were not asked to come, or they turned down the offer. I was asked by our national coach to come to this training camp. I was humbled, and I gladly accepted his offer. Let me tell you I was blessed to be here. Although I don't deserve it, God has been gracious to me. I am very thankful for the gifts he has given me!

One morning before practice as the wrestlers were warming up, I was thanking God for being here in the awesome environment. I told Him that I did not think I belonged here. He reminded me of Hebrews chapter 11.

The author of this book mentions the real heroes of our faith; "There were those who, under torture, refused to give in and go free, preferring something better: resurrection. Others braved abuse and whips, and, yes, chains and dungeons. We have stories of those who were stoned, sawed in two, murdered in cold blood; stories of vagrants wandering the earth in animal skins, homeless, friendless, powerless—the world didn't deserve them!—making their way as best they could on the cruel edges of the world" (Hebrews 11:35-37, THE MESSAGE).

I was then reminded that I too was not worthy of my brothers who went before me. They put their lives on the line for their faith. These were the real heroes who trusted God even unto death.

And yet I was on the same team—God's team. Why? Because He invited me to come into His Kingdom, then I accepted His invitation to come into my life. I wasn't recruited because of any great personal statistics or accomplishments. He just wanted me for who I was.

Let me tell you, I am continually blessed. Oh yes, there has been suffering, adversity, and hardships. But I know without a doubt God is in control. Although I don't deserve being on His team, God has been gracious to me. I am thankful for His training, and I am thankful for the gift of eternal life he has given me!

PERFORMANCE PRINCIPLE 5

LIKE A MIST

It all started about 67 years ago. My grandfather and his brother were avid Philadelphia Athletic baseball fans. The great Jimmy Foxx was their favorite player. Foxx, who was a big man in his day with a six-foot, 195 pound frame, could hit the long ball. He hit a total of 534 home runs in his career. I can recall my grandfather telling me about seeing Foxx hammer the ball over the center-field scoreboard in old Comisky Park in Chicago. Let me tell you—that would be a considered a long way in any era.

In 1936, Jimmy Foxx was traded to the Boston Red Sox for two rather mediocre athletes and $150,000. That transactions between Connie Mack of the Athletics and Tom Yawkey of the Red Sox assured that all my future family members would now be die-hard Red Sox fans.

I grew up hearing the tales of taking road trips on the train in the 1950s with the Red Sox, staying at the same hotels, going to the games, and the stories of the great Ted Williams. As a kid we went to a lot of games in Chicago to see Boston play; night games, day games, and double-headers. If we couldn't go to the game we listened to it on the radio.

The Red Sox was our team. In 1967, when I was ten years old I claimed them. I studied them with a passion: names, batting order, number, and positions. I knew the 1967 American League Championship team like no other kid outside of New England.

Rico Petrocelli, Mike Andrews, George Scott, Jose Santiago,

Carl Yastremski, Tony Conigliaro, Ken Harrelson, Reggie Smith, Dalton Jones, Jim Longborg, Jose Tartabull…even 36 years later, those are still my guys.

Some of the team members had great careers. Some like Tony Conigliaro and Jim Longborg had tremendous athletic potential, but had their careers shortened by unfortunate injuries. Others like Dan Osinski, Ken Poulsen, Norm Siebem, John Wyatt, and Joe Foy just dropped out of sight. They were gone, vanishing from the big-league diamond in an instant.

Statistics show that the average pro career in any sport is about four seasons. Many more don't make it past one year. Whether in the big leagues or here in life—our time is very, very short. James writes that we are "a mist that appears for a little while and then vanishes" (James 4:14).

Some of us may vanish in a few days, others not for many years, but the bottom line is that all of us will vanish! What remains in the end will only be that which we have done for the glory of God. Our batting average won't matter. Our championships titles won't matter. Whether we played one game or fought for 23 seasons is of little consequence. Whether "we rode the pine" or were inducted into the Hall of Fame won't matter either.

Let's focus more of our time and effort on the treasure, which will last for eternity. Let's praise Him today simply because He is God and worthy of all our praise! Make the effort, let's give the old college try to apply the truth to that which we have been given. Go and share the truth with others without shame and compromise. Accept the responsibility, take charge, and take a stand to honor and glorify God in all that you do. Being a living witness to the truth is what gets you into God's Hall of Fame. Don't let it go like a mist; make it last for eternity.

PERFORMANCE PRINCIPLE 6

UNDER CONTROL

Wayne Gretzky is referred to as the Great One. The greatest player in hockey history was nearly unbelievable in his 20-year professional career on the ice. Gretzky, a 10-time scoring champion and a nine-time MVP owns or shares a total of 61 National Hockey League records! Gretzky did things that other great players never dreamed about doing.

How he did it with no size, and a slightly above-average speed and shot is confounding to many. He did it with guile, with imagination, with instinct, with amazing intelligence, and with self-control.

What Gretzky did was indescribable. Without getting into it too deeply, suffice to say that he didn't merely break records; he destroyed them! If you can, imagine Barry Bonds having six or seven seasons where he consistently hit in the .350s and drove in 175 runs while stealing 50 bases. That might be comparable to what the Great One did on the ice if you can comprehend it.

Gretzky, who is the greatest player ever to play hockey professionally, did it without the scandals and public ego that has dominated modern sports. In fact, can you ever remember Gretzky in a fight or in the penalty box?

"He's in many ways remained the boy next door," said Cam Cole, a sports columnist in Edmonton. "You can count the times he ever said anything even slightly intemperate on the finger of one hand." ESPN commentator Barry Melrose said, "When you grow up and see a great player, you hope he's a great guy off the ice. You hope he walks what he talks, and Wayne does that." That tribute makes you want to stop and consider your own behavior in sporting events, and in the game of life as well. Amid the daily pressure and confrontations, how do I react to people at school, work, and at home, or even around town? Are my words and actions consistent?

It is clear from Gods playbook, the Bible, that God places great value on self-control. "Better a patient man than a warrior, a man who controls his temper than one who takes a city," (Proverbs 16:32). A patient person receives greater commendations than a powerful warrior. A person whose temper is under control rates higher marks than a conquering hero.

One fruit of the Spirit listed in Galatians 5:23 is self-control. This quality enables us to stay composed and focused when anger flares all around us. And that is one of the biggest victories we could ever win.

PERFORMANCE PRINCIPLE 7

WHAT CAN YOU DO?

Like so many kids today, Doug Blevins had a dream of being a sports hero, but cerebral palsy denied him his dream. Confined to a wheelchair, Blevins showed his intense determination, and refocused his sights on a new dream.

"I knew I would never play a down," said Blevins. "But I was set on this goal of making it to the National Football League."

Doug Blevins jotted down notes from every football game he watched on TV. He attended coaching camps and clinics, and studied game film with obsession. Blevins started his coaching career as a student assistant in 1982 while at the University of Tennessee. He worked with the kickers for the Volunteers for two seasons before being named the kicking coach at Emory and Henry College. A couple of years later, Blevins joined the staff at East Tennessee State. In 1988, Blevins coached high school football in Virginia before starting his own kicking consulting company in 1993. After spending a lifetime studying the game of football, Blevins became one of the top authorities on kicking a football.

In a game that often comes down to special teams, Blevins became an asset. Major colleges and the NFL were soon calling for his expertise. In 1997, Doug Blevins was hired by the Miami Dolphins as their kicking coach.

Blevins says that he has "a little cerebral palsy," and refuses to use a disability sticker on his car. He operates under this simple life philosophy, "If you stop accomplishing, you stagnate."

Unfortunately, the world is filled with people who want to take you down, down to their level. Their words are negative; you can't do that, you are too small, you're too slow, you're not smart enough, your grades aren't good enough, you don't have the talent or the ability to make it at this level, and the list can go on and on. The world is full of negative statements and negative people. Too often we believe what the world is telling us.

God tells us something that is totally different. He says, "Yes, you can!" He says, "You can do all things through Me! I will give you the strength you need," (Philippians 4:13). He says that "with me nothing is impossible," (Luke 1:37). God also says this: "For I know the plans I have for you,' declares the LORD, 'plans to prosper you and not harm you, plans to give you hope and a future. Then you will call upon me and come and pray to me, and I will listen to you. You will seek me and find me when you seek me with all your heart. I will be found by you," (Jeremiah 29:11-14).

What Doug Blevins has done was thought of as being impossible by many. What can you do with God's help?

PERFORMANCE PRINCIPLE 8

RECOGNITION

The dictionary describes recognition as the act of recognizing someone or something. In the sport of football, it is important that the quarterback has the ability to recognize the defensive alignment of the opposing team. He must be able to read it and predict the secondary coverage. Then having recognized it, it is his task to attack the weak area—the zones that are being defended inadequately. Often he might recognize that a blitz is coming. The quarterback has to get rid of the ball quickly in order to avoid being hit with a big loss. His team will gain or lose ground based on his ability to recognize what the other team is up to.

Recognition is a skill for the quarterback that comes by spending countless hours studying game films and by repeated repetitions on the practice field. Recognition helps the quarterback understand and deal with the many situations he faces during the course of a game. This important ability allows the quarterback to overcome the attack and persevere under intense pressure.

Life can be like a blitzing defense. Problems surround us at times. When the blitz comes in life, it comes at full speed—often when we are operating in slow motion. The problems you face today will either tackle you for a loss or develop you into a champion who overcomes.

Serious injuries, being benched, losses in competition, and job dismissals all take a toll on us, and it hurts! When you invest and sacrifice much, the setbacks, disappointments, and losses take a big chunk out of your heart. Taking a sack is painful, and at times it is hard to get back up off the turf where the lineman buried you—let alone pop back up and being ready to execute the next play with a clear head, agility, and grace.

Unfortunately, most of us fail to see how God wants to use problems of adversity for good in our lives. Too often we react foolishly and resent such problems rather than calling a quick time-out to consider what benefit the problem might bring.

Here are five ways God uses the blitz to get our attention:

God uses problems and adversity to *direct you.* Sometimes God must light a fire under you to get you moving. Problems often point us in a new direction and motivate us to change. Is God trying to get your attention? "Blows and wounds cleanse away evil, and beating purge the inmost being," (Proverbs 20:30).

God uses problems and adversity to *inspect you.* People are like tea bags. If you want to know what's inside them, just drop them into hot water! Has God tested your faith with a problem? What do problems reveal about you? "Consider it pure joy, my brothers, whenever you face trials of many kinds, because you know that the testing of your faith develops perseverance," (James 1:2-3).

God uses problems and adversity to *correct you.* Some lessons we learn only through pain and failure. It's likely that as a child, your parents told you not to touch a hot stove. But you probably learned by being burned. Sometimes we only learn the value of something like health, discipline, sacrifice, money, or friendship by losing it. "It was good for me to be afflicted so that I might learn your decrees," (Psalm 119:71).

God uses problems and adversity to *protect you.* A problem can be a blessing in disguise if it prevents you from being harmed by something more serious. There was a story of a man not long ago that was fired for refusing to do something unethical that his boss asked him to do. His unemployment was a problem, but it saved him from being convicted and sent to prison a year later when the actions of his former company's management were eventually discovered. "You intended to harm me, but God intended it for good to accomplish what is now being done," (Genesis 50:20).

God uses problems and adversity to *perfect you.* Problems, when responded to correctly, are character builders. God is far more interested in your character than your comfort. Your relationship to God and your character are the only two things you are going to take with you into eternity. "Not only so, but we also rejoice in our suffering, because we know that suffering produces perseverance; perseverance, character; and character, hope," (Romans 5:3-4).

Here's the bottom line: God is at work in your life, even when you don't recognize it or understand it. Like picking up a blitz, recognition is important. True and lasting success in this life is dependent on "recognizing *someone* and *something.*"

Recognition is acknowledging and accepting a loving God who sent His only Son to die for you (John 3:16). Recognition is knowing that God uses problems and adversity to develop you into the champion He knows you can be. Life is much easier and much more profitable when you have recognition!

PERFORMANCE PRINCIPLE 9

TOUGHEN UP

Steve Fraser, the national Greco-Roman wrestling coach in the United States taught a workshop at the US Olympic Committee's Sport Psychology Department and Athletes Service Division on Mental Toughness. Mental toughness is one of Coach Fraser's favorite topics of discussion.

Toughness is by definition, to be strong and resilient, able to withstand great strain without tearing or breaking.

Coach Fraser believes that by putting athletes in adverse practice situations they can learn to overcome and win! He teaches his athletes to compete in a variety of adverse situations such as being behind in the score, being a victim of a bad call by a referee, and wrestling while your opponent is cheating. Coach Fraser's philosophy is that the more you can learn to overcome, the better the training.

The toughness that Fraser preaches is learned; make no mistake about it! If you are not tough, it just means you need more practice. Just like learning or perfecting a new skill or technique, toughness can be learned, refined, and honed.

No matter how old or young, weak or strong, you can be tougher! An athlete must never believe that he can't achieve because he is not talented enough, smart enough, or because he wasn't given the gifts necessary to succeed. According to Coach Fraser, an athlete's future is much more dependent on what decisions he makes, rather than on their genetic makeup.

In a conversation with God, the prophet Jeremiah complained about the wicked and evil in the world. God responded by telling Jeremiah to toughen up. "If you have raced with the men on foot and they have worn you out, how can you compete with horses? If you stumble in safe country, how will you manage in the thickets by the Jordan?" (Jeremiah 12:5).

Life, at times, can be extremely tough. Jeremiah was crying out to God for some relief. But God's reply, in effect, was, "If you think this is bad, how are you going to cope when it gets really tough?"

God expects us to get going when the going gets tough. There are times when the load is heavy and the road is bumpy and the travel is entirely uphill. There is a time when you have to just suck it up and press on. Quitting is never an option. It is a time to refocus on Him. It is a time to praise Him for the training He is putting you through. For His training plan holds eternal value (1 Timothy 4:8).

It is also important to know that God will never put too much weight on the bar for you lift. He places the perfect amount of stress to develop the spiritual muscle we need to develop to succeed in the game. We are never left to train alone. God is there to spot us and to encourage us in the difficult sticking points.

Are you tough enough to live for Him? Are you tough enough to stand for Him? I hope you are. If not, you really need to toughen up! My prayer is that you learn how to overcome and win with the power of Christ in your life!

PERFORMANCE PRINCIPLE 10

USE IT OR LOSE IT

Daryl Strawberry had a gift for playing baseball. A Los Angles native with a ripped 6-foot-six inch physique, Daryl had a sweet swing that kept pitchers up at night. Strawberry was the 1983 National League Rookie of the Year, and he helped the New York Mets to a World Series title in 1986. Strawberry was on track to a Hall of Fame career, but along the way Strawberry developed an addiction to drugs and alcohol.

The addiction grew out of control, and Daryl Strawberry was suspended from Major League Baseball. Not only did Strawberry find himself being arrested, but he also had to deal with treatment, counseling, probation, and finally jail.

His life and baseball career took a downward spiral. Somehow the opportunity to use his gift for baseball wasn't that important to him. Over time, his poor decisions allowed what would have been a record-breaking career to die.

Daryl really made some poor decisions. But many of us make similar decisions without realizing it. It is easy to waste an amazing gift: the gift of athletic ability, the gift of academic ability, the gift of friends, the gift of speed, or strength, or whatever God has blessed you with. These gifts may not sound that dramatic, but one day at a time, making the wrong decisions, you can fritter away these gifts, and then these God-given blessings are gone from your life.

We all have done it. We make one little decision, perhaps we decide to sleep late, to blow off a practice or a workout, to have a few beers, or to eat one more piece of pizza. Suddenly we realize that we are not in the place we were once before. Each poor decision has taken us closer to the valley, rather than to the summit where we desire to be.

It is so easy to take an amazing gift and waste it. Jesus makes some strong statements about using your gift or talents in Matthew 25:14-30. He says that you would be wise and blessed to develop your talent. In fact, you will be given even more if you do so; but as for the slacker—he will have his gift taken away from him!

We need to be wise. Whatever gift you have, develop it to the max. It is a precious gift. We don't have days to waste. God gave Daryl Strawberry a gift of baseball and he threw it all away. Take the time now to cherish, enhance and nurture those talents. You will never be disappointed if you do.

PERFORMANCE PRINCIPLE II

BACK TO BASICS

In the 1996 Summer Olympic Games in Atlanta, I had the opportunity to work in the "Results" area for both the Greco-Roman and freestyle wrestling competitions. Part of our responsibility was to assign the officials and wrestlers to a specific mat for their match. We prepared the bout sheets; then following the event, we recorded the results into our computer system. Within minutes, the information we processed would be available to a worldwide audience.

For the very first time, the scoring of each bout was computerized. The bout sheet not only told the score, but also the scoring technique used and when, at which point during the match that each wrestler scored those points.

During the final Olympic medal presentations I printed out all 360 bout sheets for the matches that had been wrestled in the freestyle competition. I took those results home with me, taking apart and analyzing all the scoring maneuvers used and the time during the match when the scoring occurred. I tapped into a wealth of information—a real gold mine!

I found that the most successful takedown techniques were the single leg, the double leg, and the go-behind. All of these were basic, fundamental techniques that any first-year wrestler would learn. At the highest and most elite level of wrestling, it was the basic techniques that achieved scoring success. The same is true in all sports. Football Hall of Fame coach Vince Lombardi said of football that it is a game of blocking and tackling. It is not the formations nor the plays that win, but the best execution of the fundamentals.

Too often we turn to the latest, dazzling, and intricate strategies rather than the old familiar routine of the fundamentals.

Life is like that too. We long for something new and different, but in reality the most effective thing is what we know and have been taught from the beginning—the basics.

It is the same with our walk with Christ. Sometimes we seek a bigger church, one that has many different programs and ministries, or the one with the best music with the hope that it will draw us closer to God. Programs, facilities, and music all have their place, but they may not be the answer to our yearning.

However, what does work time and again is the fundamentals—the foundation of our faith. The basics must be drilled and practiced each day until they become a part of us. What are the basics?

Spending time with God in prayer.
Learning of God's love by daily Bible reading and study.
Living a life as a servant.
Putting our faith to work.
Loving our neighbor as ourselves.

You don't need the fun and flashy to give you direction and guidance. For all the good they do, it won't be found by following the best coaches, transferring into the best program, by attending a highly touted camp or clinic, or by following some new technique. True success in life is only found in the basic tenants of the faith just mentioned, and by the consistently following through with them. These are the rocks upon which to build your house.

Jesus said, "Therefore everyone who hears these words of mine and puts them into practice is like a wise man who builds his house on the rock," (Matthew 7:24). If you put the basics into practice, you'll remain consistent in your performance.

PERFORMANCE PRINCIPLE 12

GAZING AT OUR HEART

Recruiting is a necessary evil in collegiate athletics. Most of the rules coaches have to abide by today in the NCAA rulebook come from coaches who were relentless in their recruiting. They would do whatever it took to sign a blue-chip prospect.

There have been many athletes I have seen and recruited that had that special aura. It may be height or weight or just the look in their eyes. It may be the broadness of the shoulders, the "V" of their trunk, or just how they walk and carry themselves. The physical stature is the first thing coaches look at. The visual image plays an initial role in pursuing an athlete.

I can remember coaching huge offensive lineman that were 6-foot-4 and over 270 pounds who didn't have the heart, desire, the coordination, or the ability to excel on a football field. You thought to yourself, *Man, what a gift of size and strength. For sure I can coach him up and make him into a fine athlete.* But the sad truth is you cannot create the hunger to excel, or coach heart. You cannot buy a heart, or have it transplanted. It is simply a gift from God. It is such a sad sight to see such a spectacle—an athlete without heart!

Perhaps the toughest guy I ever coached was Keith Schneider. Keith was five foot something, 185 pounds maybe, and started at right guard on a NCAA II football team. Keith was not my idea of a starting guard—not even on the high school freshman team! But Keith proved himself day in and day out in practice. There was nothing Keith couldn't do except be big.

During Keith's senior year we threw the football 490 times in 10 games and led the nation in passing offense, and Keith did not give up one quarterback sack the entire season. What Keith didn't have was size (there isn't much you can do about that), but what Keith did have was heart and grit. He was a bulldog with an attitude!

There was a time in Israel when they longed for a king (1 Samuel 8:20). God gave them exactly what they wanted. Saul was "An impressive young man without equal among the Israelites," (1 Samuel 9:2).

Saul looked like a blue-chip athlete. He was impressive in size and stature and was loved by people, but unfortunately he failed to obey God's commands. After several years, God rejected Saul as king and sent Samuel to anoint a new king from among the sons of Jesse. When Samuel arrived at Jesse's home, he saw Eliab and thought for sure he was to be the next king (Eliab was tall and strong in stature, much like Saul).

"But the Lord said to Samuel, 'do not consider his appearance or his height, for I have rejected him. The LORD does not look at the things man looks at. Man looks at the outward appearance, but the LORD looks at the heart," (1 Samuel 16:7).

Samuel assumed the next king would be impressive to the eye, but this king would be chosen according to God's standard. God chose David, just a boy, because of his heart. David was a man who sought the heart of God and consequently had a pure heart himself.

How often do we fall into the trap of evaluating others based on outward appearance alone?

Unfortunately, much of our life is focused on being extremely impressive. We desire to have the right looks, the right credentials, and the right possessions. We long to be accepted. But in reality, God looks past the external and gazes directly into the innermost part of our heart. Our focus needs to be on how we are viewed in the eyes of God. David said, "Create in me a pure heart, O God," (Psalm 51:10).

The sad thing is, there are few things in life that have eternal value. The priorities that occupy our life become our treasure and shape and mold the condition of our heart. "Where your treasure is, there your heart will be also," (Matthew 6:21).

Let's keep our treasures firmly in the hand of God. Let's begin to consider our true appearance as we stand before a holy God. We need to seek godly standards in every area of our lives. The truth is that everything external will one day fade away— and we will stand alone with God gazing at our heart. What will He see?

PERFORMANCE PRINCIPLE 13

ESSENTIAL PURPOSE

Tammy was a very talented cross-country runner. She had all the character qualities of a champion: strong work ethic, self-discipline, and commitment.

Although Tammy wasn't the most talented individual on the team, she refused to finish second in any segment of practice. Tammy was always pushing the pace to lead and finish first. But in actual competition, it was a different story. Tammy was always back in the pack—sometimes way back.

I tried the best of my coaching wisdom on her. I worked on relaxation, then activation, self-talk, and focus. We worked on strategies and tactics for the race. We emphasized pace. Nothing worked, and I was totally frustrated. Then prior to our biggest race of the season, Tammy came to me and said, "Coach, I don't want to run this weekend."

My jaw dropped in amazement, and I asked, "Why Tammy?"

"I like to run for fun," she said. "I like training. It keeps me in shape. I like running with other people, but I don't enjoy running to win." In reality she just wanted to be a part of a running club.

What Tammy lacked was the essential purpose of a race—striving to win. Tammy is no different than a lot of people around us, including ourselves, who don't want to make the difficult effort to achieve one's full potential. Paul wrote, "Remember that in a race everyone runs, but only one person gets the prize. You also must run in such a way that you will win. All athletes practice strict self-control. They do it to win a prize that will fade away, but we do it for an eternal prize. So I run straight to the goal with a purpose in every step," (1 Corinthians 9:24-26, NLT).

Winning a race requires purpose and discipline. Paul uses this illustration to explain that the Christian life takes hard work, self-denial, and grueling preparation. As Christian athletes, we are running toward our heavenly reward—that is our essential purpose.

The requirements of proper training in the Christian life include countless repetitions of prayer, Bible study, and worship. These necessary components of the "eternal life" training program equip us to run with intensity, focus, and endurance. The training prepares us to win.

Too many people just show up for the comradery. Others just watch from the sidelines. Don't just show up to practice—do it to win! Training diligently; your spiritual performance depends on it!

PERFORMANCE PRINCIPLE 14

THE BEAUTY OF THE GAME

A lot of athletes make excuses. One season when trying to overcome a difficult run of bad luck, the place kicker for the Dallas Cowboys was asked why he missed an important field goal. "I was too busy reading my stats on the scoreboard," he told reporters.

After he missed another attempt for three points, the kicker told the media that the stadium's grass was just "too tall."

In another game, this athlete was quoted as saying, "My helmet was too tight and it was squeezing my brain." Once he even blamed his place-holder saying that he placed the ball upside down!

It is human nature to make excuses when life doesn't go our way. In my 24 years of coaching I have heard almost every possible type of excuse there is. I once heard from a very superstitious collegiate wrestler that he lost his match because he left his lucky "PEZ" candy dispenser in his locker! Oh, wow!

The apostle Paul writes to the Romans that none of us has an excuse when it comes to recognizing God. All of us Paul explains have witnessed Him.

"For since the creation of the world God's invisible qualities—his eternal power and divine nature—have been clearly seen, being understood from what has been made, so that man are without excuse" (Romans 1:20).

What Paul is saying is that God is there all around us. We just need to wake up and be attentive. God's beauty can be clearly seen around us. His touch is everywhere; you can even see it in the beauty of the game.

If you can't see the beauty in Barry Bond's swing, or in the magic of Barry Sander's cuts at the line of scrimmage, or in the intensity and focus of Lance Armstrong bouncing back after a fall, or in the awe inspiring effort of Brett Favre trying to make something out of nothing on the football field, the magnificence of a team in the struggle to overcome, or the bond of friendship forged under the pressure of reaching a common goal, then you've completely missed the beauty of God's creation in sport.

If you missed the beauty, the magic, the intensity, the love; then you missed Him too.

Paul continues saying, "For although they knew God, they neither glorified him as God nor gave thanks to him, but their thinking became futile and their foolish hearts were darkened. Although they claimed to be wise, they became fools. They exchanged the truth of God for a lie, and worshiped and served created things rather than the Creator" (Romans 1:21-22, 25).

It is a sad fact that too many people today worship the game rather than the Creator. The finger pointing, trash talking, "look at me" hotshots have indeed become fools, and in the process they have led many fans into their camps. The camp of self-gratification is found just down the dead end road of pleasure on the way to hell.

It is refreshing to see a contrast to the way the world is going. After hitting three home runs and setting a major league record by hitting a grand slam from each side of the plate, including nine RBIs in a single game, it was a pleasure to hear Bill Mueller of the Boston Red Sox honor the Creator. Mueller said in an ESPN live interview, *"I was seeing the ball real well tonight. It was an honor to set a major league record, but I just hope that this gave glory to Him."*

As you take to the field, court, mat, or pool it is my prayer that your eyes will be open to see the Author who created the beauty of the game. Embrace Him, and give Him *all the glory* with your performance.

PERFORMANCE PRINCIPLE 15

A MATTER OF INTEGRITY

Major league baseball Hall of Famer Ted Williams, of the Boston Red Sox, is arguably one of the greatest hitters to ever step onto a baseball diamond. Williams had one of his greatest seasons at the age of 39 in 1957, hitting .383 to become the oldest player ever to lead the major leagues in hitting. To prove it was no fluke, Williams led the league in the same category again in 1958, now at the age of 40, hitting .328, which was 16 percentage points below his lifetime average.

That same year, when he was toward the end of his brilliant career with Boston, he was suffering from a pinched nerve in his neck, which affected his performance. *It was so painful that he had difficulty turning his head to look at the pitcher.* At the time he was the highest paid player in any sport making $125,000 a year. As the season following the 1958 season approached, the Red Sox sent him the same contract stipulating the same amount of salary again for the upcoming season.

"When I got it, I sent it back with a note. I told them I wouldn't sign it until they gave me the full cut allowed. I never had any problem with them (the Boston management) about money. Now they were offering me a contract I didn't deserve. And I only wanted what I deserved," said Williams.

The 16 percentage points below his lifetime average was not his best, so he felt he didn't deserve to receive the maximum salary again in the upcoming season. Williams cut his own yearly salary by $31,250! Can you imagine an athlete or businessman doing that today? That's integrity!

Integrity is defined as adherence to moral and ethical principles, soundness of moral character, honesty. We live in a world turned upside down by the business scandals of Enron, WorldCom, and Anderson Consulting. In sports it is now routine to have broken contracts, demands for trades, holdouts, and a steady stream of athletic probations handed down by the NCAA. The world is searching for integrity of character.

God showed Adam the boundary line in the Garden of Eden, "You are free to eat from any tree in the garden; but you must not eat from the tree of knowledge," (Genesis 2:16-17). God has also shown each of us the boundary line between right and wrong—we know the truth in our hearts. God's line is not subject to our control, and we are not given the freedom to cross it based on how we evaluate our own special circumstances or perceived benefits.

We constantly deceive ourselves by simple justifications—rationalizations—such as, "I know this appears to be wrong, but...(you fill in the blank!)."

It is God's desire that we trust Him with all of our heart and follow His path each and every day without any shortcuts or excuses. We face numerous decisions—many places where the path divides and we must make up our minds in regard to which path is ordained by God.

Fortunately, we can depend on God to show us what we should do. It's really pretty simple—there is never any room for sin to be a part of accomplishing His perfect will. This truth will greatly simplify our decision making. If a path contains something that violates His commands, we can be sure it is not God's path.

Our integrity begins with trusting God to completely direct our every step. As we draw closer to God, all deception is exposed. Let's walk without compromise and refuse to cross God's boundary line of truth. Let's walk a straight line honestly.

As we do, we become a light that shines brightly before a world lost in darkness. Your life will count for much if you consistently practice integrity.

PERFORMANCE PRINCIPLE 16

ALWAYS READY

Jim Dowd is a thirteen-year veteran of the National Hockey League, who now is playing with the Minnesota Wild. The six-foot-one-inch, 190 pound center was never the kind of player who was denied much ice time.

Two years ago, Dowd played on the top line with the special teams. This season Dowd's playing time has been drastically reduced by Wild head coach, Jacques Lemaire. In fact, just recently Dowd saw the ice for the first time in five games. Mostly, Dowd has been centering the Wild's "crash line" with the help of a couple of rookies. He has one goal among six points and hasn't scored since the opening night of the season.

Dowd has played with six teams in his thirteen-year career and is familiar with moving around the depth chart.

"I've been on the first line, the fourth line; I've penalty killed. My whole career's been like that," said Dowd. "Whether you get five or ten shifts a night, you just have to make them good ones. It's a long season, and sometimes it's the third or fourth line that makes the difference in a game, so you have to be ready."

Jim Dowd has an attitude that coaches love! It is an attitude of selflessness and the good of the team rather than about "me."

The apostle Paul was coaching a rookie named Timothy in his first ministry position. Paul wrote this to him, "Preach the Word; be prepared in season and out of season; correct, rebuke and encourage—with great patience and careful instruction," (2 Timothy 4:2).

These instructions given almost 2000 years ago still ring true today. Paul gives us this charge to follow. We too are to be ready—at all times as Christians to share the Gospel message of hope, forgiveness, and the reconciliation of sin by the shedding of His blood on the cross. It is a message that must be proclaimed verbally, as well as visually, based on how we live our lives. We have the message of truth. It is our assignment to proclaim and live the Word before a watching world.

I like how Paul says, "be prepared in season and out of season." He is talking to those of us in the sports world. As athletes and coaches, that is exactly how we define a year—as in the in-season and the off-season. What Paul is saying is that you cannot just "chill" in the off-season, that in fact, there is no off-season when you are playing on God's team. You must work just as hard as you do during your athletic season to get the Word out to people who don't know the truth about Christ who is Savior, and King.

Being a Christian is a 24/7 assignment straight from the Master's playbook. He expects us to get the job done, whether we play on the first line, the fourth line, or just on special teams. Whatever our role is, He is counting on us to do the job for Him and to give our maximum effort. It could be you alone who could make the difference in someone's life. A simple word of encouragement or a word of instruction or a word of correction spoken in love could be the difference between eternal life and death for someone God loves.

It is your shift now. Don't take the playing time lightly and coast through your shift. You need to bust it hard and play all out. The season is long and the game is tough. You be the one to make the difference. Rise to the occasion. Be always ready, because sometimes there are opportunities to touch the lives of others when you least expect it.

PERFORMANCE PRINCIPLE 17

EFFECTIVE COMMUNICATION

The professional football dynasty of the 1960s belonged to the Green Bay Packers. The Packers won NFL championship titles in five of seven seasons. They also won the first two NFL versus AFL Championship games before the title Super Bowl existed. Two men accounted for much of this success: the legendary head coach Vince Lombardi, and All-Pro quarterback Bart Starr, both now inducted into the National Football League Hall of Fame in Canton, Ohio.

Bart Starr, surprisingly, called about 90 percent of the plays for the Green Bay offense. Starr said that he spent so much time with Lombardi on the field, in offensive strategy meetings, and in quarterback meetings, that he knew what Lombardi wanted no matter what the situation or circumstance. The key to the success of the Green Bay Packer offense was Coach Lombardi communicating plays, formations, situations, down and distance options, and defensive keys into Bart Starr's mental playbook. Recognition came as a series of success versus the opposition's defense repeatedly distinguished the offense.

Communication is essential to building and maintaining any relationship. As we walk down the path God lays before us, we soon discover there are many forks in the road—decision points where we must choose between God's play selection and manipulating our own moves in the world. At these critical moments, we must be able to recognize the guidance of our Master Coach as given through His Spirit. If we have not spent sufficient time with Him in His Word and communicating in prayer, we cannot expect to understand His play calling in our time of greatest need.

David wrote, "Give ear to my words, O Lord, consider my sighing. Listen to my cry for help my King and my God, for to you I pray in the morning, O Lord, You hear my voice; in the morning I lay my request before you and wait in expectation," (Psalm 5:1-3).

David states that the morning is his dedicated time for prayer; his time to be alone with God, to share his heart and expectantly await God's direction. But God has not specified a preferred time for prayer. In fact, Paul encourages us to maintain a constant state of communication with God when he says to "pray continuously," (1 Thessalonians 5:17). We ought to strive for communication which is regular and frequent—any time is the right time for prayer!

The important thing is that prayer must originate from a sincere heart, anything less becomes just babble. We should be motivated by a desire to strengthen our relationship, to praise Him for His blessings, and earnestly ask for His guidance—and to deepen the commitment of our love. We ought to value our time with God above anything else this world has to offer. "One thing I ask the LORD, this is what I seek; that I may dwell in the house of the LORD all the days of my life," (Psalm 27:4).

Let's make sure our devotion doesn't fade. Let's set aside time each day to be alone with God—time to hear His voice, time for Him to guide our play selection. We can't go into this game of life alone without His guidance and wisdom. It takes time and communication with the Master Coach to be effective. Effective communication starts on your knees and ends with Him ensuring success.

PERFORMANCE PRINCIPLE 18

HOLDING BACK

In my athletic and coaching career, I have seen many athletes being held back from realizing their true potential. Something, someone weighed them down, held on and tugged on their jersey, not allowing them to perform at full speed.

There are countless factors outside the arena that slow down performance. It can be a boyfriend/girlfriend relationship. It can be friends who don't understand or appreciate your goals, and your personal need for sacrifice and commitment, who pull you into parties and other counterproductive situations. It can be alcohol and drugs. It can be demanding parents or parents who don't have any expectations. It can be academics. It can be the fear of failure or a subconscious aversion to success. It can be as simple as a lack of discipline, or it can be stress and anxiety. It can be someone's cruel words, which say you will never be good enough. The list of factors that hamper individual performance can be endless.

I have seen too many athletes leave their sport with regrets. "I wish I would have. I wish I could have. I wish I should have." Something held them back from giving it their all, from reaching the next level of performance and achievement.

Think for a moment. What is holding you back from being the best you can be?

Living a life free of regret is difficult. Everyday we are bombarded with things that attempt to pull us away from God and steal our joy. At times we may wonder why God makes it so difficult to follow Him. But God didn't create the difficulty. The world system has produced barriers at every turn—barriers that can only be overcome through faith.

We must continually believe the truth of His Word and allow our faith to mature by taking steps, which lead us closer to God, even if our steps of faith seem like baby steps. With each new step, we more clearly see the truth of God's promises; we begin to see past the visible to "him who is invisible," (Hebrews 11:27). We continue to draw near until we finally take the step into total commitment.

In Psalms, David wrote, "Into your hands I commit my spirit; redeem me, O LORD, the God of truth," (Psalm 31:5).

At some point in our Christian race, we must make a decision. We are either going to love by faith and trust, or we are going to live in uncertainty and fear. We either fully commit our life to God, or we continue to fight life's battles with our own limited strength and pulled by the temptations of the world and swayed by our own deceptive desires.

The author of Hebrews speaks such truth to this issue. "Therefore, since we are surrounded by such a great cloud of witnesses, let us throw off everything that hinders and the sin that so easily entangles, and let us run with perseverance the race marked out for us. Let us fix our eyes on Jesus, the author and perfecter of our faith, who for the joy set before him endured the cross, scorning its shame, and sat down at the right hand of the throne of God. Consider him who endured such opposition from sinful men, so that you will not grow weary and lose heart," (Hebrews 12:1-3).

Run the race to win! Let nothing hold you back!

Performance Principle 19

Consider the Sacrifice

A few years ago there was a sporting goods advertisement which featured three-time NCAA I champion and 1999 World Freestyle Wrestling champion, Steven Neal. Neal is quoted in the ad as saying, "My toughest match is not in the ring—it's at the dinner table and at the fast food restaurants. It's hearing about the party I can never go to. It's realizing that being a great wrestler isn't a sport, it's a life."

Steven Neal sacrificed much to reach his athletic goals. To reach the next level in any sport or endeavor requires sacrifice. Webster defines sacrifice as: "Voluntary giving up of something valued."

When God first led the Israelites out of Egypt, He warned them about following the practices of the local people who lived in the land. "You must not do as they do in the land of Canaan, where I am bringing you," (Leviticus 18:3). The ways of the world will almost always be in conflict with the ways of God.

God's chosen people not only turned their backs, they became involved in a local form of "worship" that included sacrificing their own children. It's not too different even today.

We have been blessed with family, friends, teammates, coaches, and a wonderful relationship with God through the forgiveness and sacrifice that Jesus paid for us. And yet, how often do we sacrifice these blessings to gods of this world? How often do we follow the practices of the world and burn our children or our marriage in the fire of "victory?" How often do we sacrifice our relationships on the alter of "selfish pleasure?"

Our heavenly Father is calling us to a spiritual worship of complete and total sacrifice of ourselves. "Offer your bodies as living sacrifices, holy and pleasing to God," (Romans 12:1). This sacrifice is one of continually releasing our will in order to be "poured out like a drink offering," (2 Timothy 4:6).

So how can you "offer yourself as a living sacrifice"?

You can bring out your very best to God's table by making your performance (and in fact all that you do) "a love offering of worship" to Him. When you compete for an audience of One, the stresses and temptations of the world cease. It is easy to perform your best for the One who gave His all for you. Listen to what God asks you to sacrifice; then make it one of love and pure devotion.

PERFORMANCE PRINCIPLE 20

FINISH THE RACE

I'm sort of big guy (6-foot-1, and 260 pounds), the guy who played the offensive line in football and who wrestled heavyweight. One thing big guys hate doing is running. I always hated to run. I never enjoyed wind sprints or long-distance running. It was just something you always had to do as an athlete to get into playing shape. You just had to "gut it out" and get it done. For me and many others running is a tough, but necessary challenge. It was never, ever done for fun!

Some time ago I was asked to coach our college's women's cross-country team. I was amazed how much they loved to run! They would run a mile and half for warm-up, run a six mile workout, then cool down by running another mile or two. They would giggle, laugh and just enjoy the greatest time together. I was, and still am, blown away by what they do and the attitude they always possessed. But this group is a real exception to the rest of us!

Paul talks about God's race in the Bible. His race is long and often difficult; there are many distractions that slow us down and even pull us away from the finish line—at times we may even wonder why we are running. But being a participant in God's eternal race is infinitely more rewarding than standing on the sidelines and watching the runners go by!

Paul said, "I consider my life worth nothing to me, if only I may finish the race and complete the task the LORD Jesus had given me—the task of testifying to the gospel of God's grace," (Acts 20:24).

Several years later Paul wrote, "I have learned the secret of being content in any and every situation," (Philippians 4:12). When facing hardships, the tough race, the wind in his face, and with side stitches, Paul showed he had already learned the secret of running the race. No matter what the circumstances of life, Paul knew his contentment was based on bringing glory and honor to God. His life had a wonderful purpose even in the face of great adversity and harsh training conditions.

The real race God has for us affects the deepest part of our heart, unseen in the flurry of activity. Running well is not defined by doing more; rather, we run a "successful" race when we stay focused (Hebrews 12:2), keep our race pace (Hebrews 12:1), and run the race plan that the Master Coach has set for us (James 1:2).

We must continue to run with all the strength God provides, and when our strength fades, we must run within the protection of His grace and His strength. Let's run with the motivation of bringing Him glory and honor by loving Him with *all* of our heart, soul, mind, and strength—and let's continue to run with a burning desire to finish the race in a fashion most pleasing to the Lord.

PERFORMANCE PRINCIPLE 21

SUPREME SACRIFICE

Greg Ostertag's greatest assist never appeared in a basketball box score. It didn't even help win a game either. Ostertag helped save his sister's life. The Utah Jazz center made a supreme sacrifice this summer, risking his NBA playing career and his own health by donating a kidney to his younger sister, who has diabetes.

One of the NBA's biggest players, the seven-foot-two-inch, 280-pound Ostertag now has a four-inch scar on his stomach as a reminder of where the doctors removed the healthy kidney that is now inside his sister, Amy Hall.

Amy, who has had diabetes since she was seven years old, began having kidney problems three years ago. When her kidneys started to fail in March of 2002, a transplant was the only thing that could be planned to save her life.

Fortunately, doctors didn't have to look far to find a match. "I told her from the beginning, 'Whatever you need, give a call.' And she did in March," Ostertag said.

In a way we are all very much like Amy Hall, but instead of diabetes we suffer from a serious spiritual problem that is terminal. Our only hope is for a Savior, for someone to sacrifice what they have for what we need. But unlike Amy Hall, before we even had to ask for help in our condition, God provided a way. Paul wrote, "God demonstrates his own love for us in this: While we were still sinners, Christ died for us," (Romans 5:8).

Christ's death held great purpose in God's ultimate plan.

The apostle John wrote that, "God so loved the world (you!) that he gave his one and only Son, that whoever believes in him shall not perish but have eternal life. For God did not send his Son into the world to condemn the world, but to save the world through him," (John 3:16-17).

It is here that God sets the standard of true love, the basis for all relationships. When you love someone dearly, you are willing to give freely to the point of self-sacrifice. God paid dearly with the life of His Son, Jesus. His death on the cross was the highest price He could pay. *He did it all for you!*

In return, God wants us to offer ourselves as a "living sacrifice," (Romans 12:1) in which we daily lay aside our own desires to follow Him, putting all or our energies and resources at His disposal and trusting Him to guide us along the way, each and every day. We do this as an act of worship, of gratitude that our sins have been forgiven, paid for in the most supreme of all sacrifices.

God's love is so great for you! Can you imagine the cost of the gift He gave you?

Now is the time to receive the gift. Now is the time to be thankful for His sacrifice. Now is the time to be that living sacrifice. Do it for Him. That is the supreme sacrifice He desires from you.

PERFORMANCE PRINCIPLE 22

PLEASURE OR PAIN

Chariots of Fire, the fact-based, Oscar winning movie depicts the quest of Harold Abrahams and Eric Liddell to win Gold medals in the 1924 Olympics, a feat they both accomplished.

With about an hour before the final heat in the 400-meter race, while his trainer was giving him a massage, Harold Abrahams laments to his best friend, "I'm 24 and I've never known contentment. I'm forever in pursuit, and I don't even know what it is I'm chasing."

What is it you're chasing? Have you experienced true contentment?

Most of us have an idea what we are chasing, but when we finally capture the prize there is not the contentment in the accomplishment for which we had hoped. Instead, there is a hunger, and even deeper pain of emptiness.

The difference between Abrahams and Liddell is transparent: everything that Abrahams did was for himself, while everything Liddell did was for the glory of God.

Liddell's little sister, Jennie, mistook her brother's love of running for rebellion against God, and pressed him to return to the mission field in China where they were born, and their parents lived. Catching her arms, trying to explain his calling to run he said, "Jennie, Jennie. You've got to understand. I believe God made me for a purpose—for China. But He also made me fast! And when I run, I feel His pleasure!

The secret of contentment is not getting what you want, but redefining what you need. Most people, like Abrahams, only think of what they want and are painfully disconnected. Others, like Liddell, redefine their needs, live to please God, and "feel His pleasure."

In the course of athletic competition, when the rush of adrenaline flows, when your lungs expand from the thrill of the chase, and when the rate of your pulse accelerates from the smell of victory—remember the source of such pleasure. See what you need, and be content in what God freely gives you. Enjoy His pleasure!

PERFORMANCE PRINCIPLE 23

SECURING THE VICTORY

In athletic competition, whether you are leading or behind in the closing moments, the main thing is to make sure you end up with the victory. In the 2002 World Series, we got a clinic on how to get it done.

The New York Yankees were only two outs from their fourth straight championships and the fifth in six years when the Arizona Diamondbacks somehow found a way to beat them. The Diamondbacks had, incredibly, bounced back from two of the toughest losses in World Series history. They had dropped Games 4 and 5 at Yankee Stadium, games it looked as if they were going to win.

New York's Alfonso Soriano's solo home run off of Curt Schilling put the Yankees ahead 2-1 in the eighth inning. Mariano Rivera, the most dominant reliever in postseason baseball history set down the Diamondbacks in the bottom half of the eighth.

Then in the ninth inning, Arizona rallied. Mark Grace led off with a single, and Rivera threw away Damian Miller's bunt for an error, putting runners at first and second base. Jay Bell bunted into a force play at third. Tony Womack tied up the game at 2-2 with an RBI double to the right field corner.

Craig Counsel was then hit by an inside high fastball to load the bases with one out. Luis Gonzalez came to the plate. With the infield in, Gonzalez choked up on the bat and for the first time that year, then blooped a soft single just a few feet beyond the infield dirt.

The fourth-year expansion team, playing in their first World Series, with their backs to the wall, found a way to get the win. The same is true with us. It is not how you start that matters, it is all about how you finish.

The battle we are in is not against flesh and blood, but against the authorities, against the powers of this dark world and against the spiritual forces of evil in the heavenly realms (Ephesians 6:12).

This is no afternoon athletic contest that we will walk away from and forget in a couple of hours. This is for keeps—a life-or-death fight to the finish against the Devil and all his fallen angels.

How do you make sure you end up the winner in an all-out fight such as this?

The Master Coach tells us that we are "more than conquerors" (Romans 8:37), and that "(we) can do everything through him who gives (us) strength" (Philippians 4:13), so we have the ability to secure the victory no matter what the situation or circumstance in the game of life.

The keys to victory are to follow the game plan that the Coach gives to us. We are told to "Run in such a way as to get the prize," (1 Corinthians 9:24), to "run with perseverance the race marked out for us," and to "fix our eyes on Jesus," (Hebrews 12:1-2), and to "put on the full armor of God, so that when the day of evil comes, you may be able to stand your ground," (Ephesians 6:13).

So let's not allow ourselves to get fatigued in doing good. At the proper time, we will find ourselves victorious if we don't give up or quit. So fight the good fight! Secure the victory!

PERFORMANCE PRINCIPLE 24

ALMOST PERFECT

Born on September 19, 1967 in Novosibirsk, Siberia, no one has owned the sport of wrestling like Alexander Karelin did. He made wimps out of otherwise supreme athletes—there is simply no way to verbally capture what Karelin could do physically to an opponent.

At the age of 17 Karelin became the Junior World Champion in Greco-Roman Wrestling, then dominated the world from that point on. In 1987, Alexander started an unbelievable winning streak, winning nine consecutive world championship titles and three consecutive Olympic Gold medals. This kind of domination was unheard of in wrestling, let alone any other individual sport.

Karelin's goal was to retire undefeated in international competition—and to win the Gold medal for the fourth time in the 2000 Sydney Olympics. Everything was on track, right up to the Gold medal finals where he met Rulon Gardner of the United States. Gardner was an unlikely opponent, whose best effort was awarded fifth place in the 1997 World Championships. In 13 years, Karelin had not lost a single match, and during that period of time he only allowed one single point to be scored against him. The stage was set for a perfect ending to a perfect career.

Unfortunately for Karelin, Rulon Gardner did not see it that way. Gardner battled in the match of his life, winning a 1-0 overtime decision to become the 2000 Olympic Champion. No one expected a Gardner victory, except maybe Gardner himself. The great Russian hero left the mat for the first time hanging his head, humbled in defeat.

Perfection eludes all of us. We get up in the morning determined to do the best we can today, but before we know it, we've messed up and sinned. The same thing happened to the great heroes of the Bible. We can see from the lives of the great Biblical characters how tough it was to achieve perfection. God called David, "a man after mine own heart," (Acts 13:22), yet even David fell into adultery with Bathsheba (2 Samuel 11:1-27). And Paul, the greatest missionary ever, admitted that he did what he didn't want to do (Romans 7:15).

Sadly, just like Paul, all of us fall far short of perfection. When we do, it is our responsibility to confess our sins to God and accepts His mercy. The curse of imperfection strikes often, but we can learn from it and keep on growing if we admit our mistakes in humility and honesty.

God promises to cleanse us, wash away our sins, and remember them no more. The only way for that to happen is to have a personal relationship with Him. And if we do have that relationship with Jesus as our Savior and Lord, one day we will be perfect, just as He is.

PERFORMANCE PRINCIPLE 25

NO PRESSURE

Pressure. It is a way of life in athletics. Pressure abounds: pressure to win, the pressure to make the team, the pressure to keep your position and ranking, the pressure of criticism and of fame.

Basically there are two types of pressure that an athlete will face. The first type of pressure is the kind you have control over. This type of pressure usually comes when you have failed to train and be properly prepared. It shows up when you are out of shape, whether it be your cardiovascular system, your flexibility, your strength, your weight, or your state of mind. It is not being as ready as you could be in one way or another.

This type of pressure also shows up in your preparation for competition. This usually happens when going into battle without a plan or strategy. It is going into a tough competition without doing your homework. All of this pressure is totally avoidable. The real problem is that you created this mess by not being disciplined enough to simply prepare a game plan.

The other type of pressure is unavoidable. It is beyond the sphere of your control. This type of pressure usually hits you from the outside. Its source is created by the actions of others. It is the pressure to live up to someone else's expectations. It is fear of failure, and the fear of the unknown. It can be unexpected circumstances, or even completely unrelated events. This is the kind of pressure you must learn to face because there is nothing you can do about it.

The important issue is, how are you going to deal with the pressures of life and sport? It is there, and it just won't go away on its own. You can't run and hide, and you can't pretend it is not there. You must face it. Anytime you step on the field of life, you step on a field covered with land mines of pressure. With each step, the possibility of a pressure explosion exists at every turn. So how can one hope to deal effectively with this kind of strain.

Paul wrote that, "By his mighty power at work within us, he is able to accomplish infinitely more than we would ever dare to ask or hope," (Ephesians 3:20, NLT). We overcome pressure by surrendering to the awesome ability of God. God is bigger than any pressure you face, and nothing takes Him by surprise. But you must let His power work through you.

This is a key principle. Let God be strong through you. Allow His awesome ability to do its work in your life and in the exact situation you are facing. "The eyes of the LORD search the whole earth in order to strengthen those whose hearts are fully committed to him," (2 Chronicles 16:9, NLT).

God is always around to help you deal with the stress you must face. Solomon writes in Proverbs, "there is a friend who sticks closer than a brother," (Proverbs 18:24). God is not going to desert you in the hard, pressure-packed times. He will be there for you. Would it surprise you to know that God is patiently waiting for your to trust Him with your problems, and when you do you will be blessed! (Jeremiah 17:7).

God is known by many names. There are many names for God throughout the book of Isaiah, but even more edifying are the qualities of His character that we can depend on. "And he will be called Wonderful Counselor, Mighty God, Everlasting Father, Prince of Peace," (Isaiah 9:6).

When I trust and surrender to God the pressures of my life, I am rewarded with wisdom and guidance from the Wonderful Counselor. I gain power and strength from our Mighty God, and I can stand on the rock unshaken in the storm of adversity with my Everlasting Father; and I can rest, relax and sleep at night assured because of the Prince of Peace lives in my heart.

So if pressure is eating away at your life, throw up your arms and surrender. Only when you surrender, can you find true victory—lasting peace, and NO PRESSURE.

PERFORMANCE PRINCIPLE 26

IN PURSUIT OF SPORTSMANSHIP

Legendary football coach Vince Lombardi once said that, "winning isn't everything, but making the effort to is." Today in our society as we watch professional and college sports, we can witness that making the effort to win is not important at all. Now the only thing important is winning, at any price.

"Whatever it takes" is the theme song sung by a new generation of athletes and coaches. It can embody cutting corners, behavior flagrantly lacking in sportsmanship, the use of performance-enhancing drugs, trash talking, chest bumping, in your face intimidation, and just flat-out, old-fashioned cheating. There was a day though when it mattered a great deal how a game was played. It used to be as important as winning and losing.

In the 1936 Olympic Games, Germany's Luz Long was one of the world's most elite long jumpers. Long looked forward to competing not only in the Olympics in his own country, but he dreamed of competing against the great Jesse Owens of the United States, who held the current world record. Owens, however, foot-faulted on his first two qualifying jumps. With only one more attempt left to qualify, Owens was in danger of missing the medal competition.

Long suggested that Owens make a mark several inches before the takeoff board to avoid fouling again. Jesse Owens took his advice and it worked! He qualified by a centimeter, and eventually defeated Long for the Gold medal. An athlete of today might not be so likely to take similar actions.

Sadly, from the youth leagues to the professional ranks, there has been a decline in sportsmanship. We have traded sportsmanship, which means desiring to defeat an opponent in an honorable way at his or her best, for gamesmanship. Sportsmanship, which is a desire to defeat an opponent at his best in fair-and-square competition, has been abandoned in favor of gamesmanship. We are getting to the point where winning at sport or in the business world is a matter of cleverly bending the rules—or even breaking them, as long as you don't get caught.

Gamesmanship was the agenda when college football coaches bought offensive lineman gloves to match the colors of their opponent's jerseys so that they could conceal illegal holding. Most of the rules in the NCAA rule book that college coaches have to follow are based on past actions of gamesmanship, on actions by coaches who were always searching for an edge in the shadows.

We need to pursue sportsmanship in our athletic endeavors and in business and everywhere else we travel. We need to teach it and talk about it. Those of us who get it need to model it for other coaches, athletes, teammates, and opponents. Let's live and play by the old cliché, "It's not whether you win or lose, but how you play the game."

We need athletes and coaches who are determined to take a stand to do things the way they should be done. Let's be humble in victory and gracious in defeat; let's play our hearts out no matter the situation or score; let's pick up our fallen comrades, and give honor to sport, competition, and to the God we serve.

PERFORMANCE PRINCIPLE 27

DOING THE RIGHT THING

It is almost unthinkable, yet it is the true story of Rueben Gonzales. Gonzales was a professional racquetball player. He was playing in the tournament finals for the first time on the profession circuit, and he was up against one of the best in the sport.

In the fourth and final game, at match point, Gonzales made an unbelievable "kill short" into the front wall to win the game, and the tournament. The referee called the shot good. One of the two linesmen affirmed the shot was in. But Gonzales, after a moment of hesitation, turned around, shook his opponent's hand, and declared that his final shot had "slapped: into the wall, hitting the floor before making contact with the wall. As a result, Gonzales lost the match. He walked off the court, leaving behind a stunned crowd and opponent.

In the next issue of *National Racquetball* Magazine displayed Rueben Gonzales on its front cover. The story searched for an explanation of this first occurrence on the professional racquetball circuit. Who could ever imagine something like this in any sport?

A player with victory in hand disqualifies himself at match point and lost! According to writer Dennis Waitley, when Gonzales was asked why he took this action, he said, "It was the only thing I could do and maintain my integrity."

How many times have we as athletes and coaches tried to play on the edge of the rules, doing whatever we think we can get away with to win? We argue when we are penalized, we easily point fingers at the sins of our opponents, and we get in the face of officials when they miss a call. How many times have we rejoiced silently when our opponents are penalized unjustly—when we get away with a "gift?"

God is calling us as athletes and coaches to a life of integrity and character in all that we do. Often times this worldview conflicts with God's truth. Regardless of the argument, there is only one way to do things—*God's way*. Even when we flirt in the gray areas, He sees everything, even what the referee misses.

The Bible tells us that Josiah "did what was right in the sight of the LORD," (2 Chronicles 34:2). Undoubtedly, many people criticized him bitterly for tearing down their religious shrines, but that mattered little. Josiah was more concerned about what was right in "the sight of the LORD."

Today, and every day, let's make it our aim to do what is right in the eyes or our invisible and all-important observer in heaven. You may be hammered in the media, by people on campus, by other coaches, and even by your athletes or teammates for doing what is right. That hammering only makes us stronger. What matters most is pleasing God by doing what He determines is right and just.

The Master Coach counts integrity above winning. We can treat sporting activities with love and enthusiasm, yet we should never cross the line from competitor to selfish manipulator. I encourage you to strive to have integrity in all you do, realizing that you are a winner when you don't compromise God's standards. Doing the right thing is never the wrong thing to do.

PERFORMANCE PRINCIPLE 28

LASTING SIGNIFICANCE

As a collegiate coach, I often ask a variety of athletes and coaches, "What is your greatest desire?" The answers vary, of course. Regardless of what is desired to be achieved though, whether on the court, field, pool, or the mat, most invariably speak about their desire to achieve and be somebody significant. Significance is a common denominator with most athletes and coaches. They want purpose, meaning, and fulfillment. We all do.

Some of the most frequent comments I've heard are:

"I want to be somebody."
"I want to make a contribution."
"I want to have an impact."
"I want to…conquer…achieve…or prove myself."
"I want be the best."
"I want to be a champion."
"I want to move up to the next level."
"I want to be successful."

How do you go about satisfying your need to be significant?

Most of us are eager to achieve the trophies and applause of life. We pursue significance by gratifying our own selfish ambitions. We seek the goal with intensity and primary focus, yet we let other areas of our life slide.

How we each answer the questions, "Who am I, and why do I exist?" determines how we pursue our significance. Our answers divide us into two distinct groups; those who pursue significance in lasting ways and those who pursue significance in temporary ways. Our desire to satisfy this need can take us close to, or far way from God's desire and plan for us.

Real lasting significance is found in Jesus Christ, He said, "I am the vine; you are the branches. If a man remains in me and I in him, he will bear much fruit; apart from me you can do nothing," (John 15:5-6).

Frankly, we as athletes and coaches cannot find true significance in any lasting way apart from Christ. So if you are in Christ, and submit to God's plan and purpose, then you can satisfy your greatest need in a way that endures. Otherwise all your efforts are in vain.

The greatest risk is to think about who you really are as a person in terms of the position you hold. The heartache comes when you no longer have the position, and you realize people were not really interested in you because you were you, but because of the position you held, because they thought your position could be of benefit to them.

The sad fact is that you will not always be the starter, the all-time record holder, the gold medalist, or the Coach of the Year. Memories fade, power is diminished, medals tarnish, and records are broken. Seek a true, enduring significance. Seek a personal relationship with Christ; He will never disappoint you.

If you sincerely desire a true and lasting significance, then invite Jesus Christ into your heart and into your life. We receive Christ by faith and repentance. Prayer, which is simply talking to God, is an excellent way to express faith. Here is a suggested prayer:

> Lord Jesus, I acknowledge that I have been attempting to find significance in an inappropriate way. As a result, I have sinned against You. Thank You for dying on the cross for me and forgiving my sins. As an act of faith, I invite You to come

into my life and direct me. Take control of my life, and make me into the kind of person You want me to be. Amen.

If this prayer expresses your desire, why not kneel wherever you are right now, and invite the living God to coach you in your life? True significance is found only in Jesus Christ. Apart from Him we can do nothing.

PERFORMANCE PRINCIPLE 29

PUTTING THE ARMOR ON

Mike Singletary was a terrifying linebacker in the National Football League throughout the 1980s. The former two-time All-American at Baylor University was captain of the Chicago Bears defense, and was named All-Pro ten-times while starting an amazing 172 games. In 1985, Singletary helped lead the Bears to a Super Bowl championship.

Mike Singletary was a model of consistency and toughness throughout his NFL Hall of Fame career. His continuous efforts to be—always—the best he could be earned him the respect and admiration of his teammates, coaches, and football fans everywhere.

Former San Francisco 49ers head coach George Seifert compared the Bears linebacker to yet another Hall of Famer. "Mike is the modern-day Ray Nitschke," he said. "He has set the standard for what coaches and scouts look for in inside linebackers."

Whether it was at Baylor or with Chicago, Singletary always played full out. It didn't matter if it was practice or a game, he maintained the same level of intensity. You could see the focus, the concentration in his eyes. He was ready to erupt on every snap of the ball.

Although quiet and thoughtful off the field, once Mike put on the football pads—the battle armor—he was transformed into a ferocious player on the field. He truly enjoyed the physical aspects of football and make no secret of the fact that he liked hitting the ball carrier, "I like to hit people," he once said. Singletary hit the opposition with such explosive power that he actually cracked 16 helmets during his years at Baylor. That body armor protected Mike from serious injury.

Unlike Mike and the game of football, we need to keep our armor on at all times. It isn't just for practice or for game time. Our spiritual armor is a line of defense. We need to put it on and keep it on.

Paul tells the team in Ephesus that, "Finally, be strong in the Lord and in his mighty power. Put on the full armor of God so that you can take your stand against the devil's schemes," (Ephesians 6:10-11).

The opposing team has a fast offense. It is free-spirited, reckless, and overconfident. Their offense can produce a pounding style of attack, or they can be deceptive and covert. Regardless, their attack is ruthless in the air and on the ground. The opposing coach is clever, ingenious, and deceptive. He will do whatever it takes to seek, destroy, and defeat you. And he loves to inflict pain.

If we are not prepared, focused, and ready for anything, we can take a whipping. At all times, we need to strap it up, keeping our spiritual armor on. Our armor of God is a mighty weapon that allows us to stand strong, impenetrable to the onslaught from the dark forces.

Victories aren't won without a fight. Satan will not give up on his attack. He enjoys troubling you. He will continue to pound the center of the line in hopes of gaining ground. If you are a believing Christian, the Devil hates you, and all those that play and serve on God's team are his sworn enemies.

Being on God's team, you are in the front line, but He has given you His special armor to help defend yourself.

Be determined to strap it up daily (Ephesians 6:11).
Know whose team you are on (Isaiah 41:9-10).
Talk daily to the Master Coach (Philippians 4:6-7).

Read up on how to play a victorious game in the playbook (Psalm 25:5).

Huddle up with other team members (1 John 1:7).

Recruit new members to the team (Colossians 4:3-6).

And always keep alert and focused (Hebrews 12:2).

These things are essential components in competing with a purpose.

Put on the full armor of God everyday. Fight the good fight. Win with relentless love, praise, and thanksgiving.

PERFORMANCE PRINCIPLE 30

GIVE A LESSON TO THE WORLD

Retiring International Olympic Committee president Juan Antonio Samaranch put pressure on the Athens 2004 Olympic Organizing Committee, reminding them that they have a cultural duty to put on "the best Games ever."

Eighteen months after issuing the Organizing Committee a "yellow light" and threatening that the Games may go elsewhere, Samaranch noted that things were finally going the right way in Athens.

Samaranch told the Athens Organizing Committee, "The beginning was too slow, and now have to gain the time you lost at the beginning." Samaranch continued, "You have to give the lesson to the world that you in Greece, where the games were born many centuries ago, you can organize the best Games ever."

Just as Samaranch admonished the Organizing Committee in Greece that they have a duty to host the best Olympic Games ever, so it is our duty as followers of Christ "to live a life worthy of the calling you have received," (Ephesians 4:1).

God expects us as Christian athletes and coaches to perform at a certain level. His performance standard for us is "to be completely humble and gentle; being patient, bearing with one another in love."

This standard applies to us all the time, no matter what the score is, the situation, or the circumstances. It is our obligation, our duty to model to the world the life of Christ. It is a performance principle that we cannot ignore. What's more, it is a model of behavior that the world will not fail to notice. When we do the right thing no matter what the circumstances, people cannot help but notice. Loving actions bear witness of Him who is love, and once love has been set in motion the world is changed forever.

So go out today and give a lesson to the world—a lesson of love from the Master Coach.

PERFORMANCE PRINCIPLE 31

THINK ABOUT IT

Olympic and World champion Tom Brands once said that, "Wrestling is 95 percent mental." The mental side of sport may not be 95 percent, but it does play an important part of any game. Mental skills coach Beasey Hendrix is a master of the psychological side of sport. Coach Hendrix has trained countless elite world-class athletes who desire to win the Gold. Coach Hendrix has worked with athletes on many specific areas that enhance performance, one of which is goal setting.

Coach Hendrix teaches athletes that by setting goals and measuring their achievement, they are able to see what they have done and what they are capable of doing. The process of achievement goals and seeing their achievement gives them confidence and the belief that they will be able to achieve higher and more difficult goals.

So where do you want to be in five years? How about 10 years? We are encouraged to set goals which are just beyond what we think we can reach. Then we are to create a set of short-term, intermediate, and long-term plans to accomplish these goals.While there is nothing wrong with setting goals and creating plans, we must first ask a longer-term question; where do you want to be in 100 years? Unless we grasp the significance of this question and have a solid answer, the rest of our goals will be based on a false set of criteria and are not worth pursuing. What difference does it make which college we attend or which coaching position we take if we failed to address the issue of where we will spend eternity?

Solomon wrote, "The wisdom of the prudent is to give thought to their ways, but the folly of fools is deception," (Proverbs 14:8). Do not be deceived! Even though the average life span continues to increase, life is short. An average life lasts about 45,000,000 minutes. This seems like a lot, but by this time tomorrow; 1440 minutes will be gone, and 100 years from now… "Be very careful, then, how you live—not as unwise but as wise, making the most of every opportunity because the days are evil," (Ephesians 5:15-16).

We must learn to evaluate all of our decisions and goals based on the overriding goal of living a life dedicated to God, of spending an eternity worshipping Him in Heaven. The clock continues to tick; let's give thought to our ways!

PERFORMANCE PRINCIPLE 32

SELF-EXAMINED

One of the greatest tools at the disposal of athletes and coaches is that of videotape recording. Videotape gives the athlete and coach the ability to review past competitions, and to critically evaluate the technique and performance as well as decision making skills under pressure.

If you look up *evaluate* or *examine* in a book of synonyms you'll find a list that includes *investigate, inspect, survey, probe, scrutinize, test, question, and review.* The method of study is one of the keys to improving performance for any athlete or coach.

I have a great videotape system in my office. The kind I can freeze a frame by itself or play a sequence frame-by-frame to create a super slow-motion succession of frames either in forward or reverse. This enables me to watch even the briefest details. I can evaluate many aspects of the sport which are so important to success. I also like to study our opponents and learn their tendencies and their weaknesses too!

I can clearly remember when I was a rookie coach, Bill McCartney, who was the defensive coordinator of the University of Michigan football team at the time, saying in a coaching clinic how important it was to study and evaluate any problems that come up in competition and deal with them right away. "If you don't," said McCartney, "they will come back to haunt you the very next week."

I am a firm believer in studying video. You can't watch enough, really. From video study you can learn why techniques and tactics are not working. In fact, you can see the mistakes and make the necessary adjustments. I strongly encourage our team members to study their competitors as they would if it was an academic class. I tell them that if they are committed and serious about being the best they can be, they need to study tape and continually make self-examinations of performance, not just hear it from me.

Athlete or not, we can't go through life without doing some self-evaluation on who we are and what we believe and how we are living life. It takes some guts, some personal toughness to throw up the video tape on your life on the big screen, to go beyond just watching, to digging down deep (to investigate, inspect, survey, probe, scrutinize, test, question, and review), then deal with what we find.

The Master Coach God, knows every detail of our lives; "Everything is uncovered and laid bare before the eyes of him to whom we must give account," (Hebrews 4:13). But our Master Coach desires for us to "Examine yourself to see whether you are in the faith; test yourselves," (2 Corinthians 13:5).

Just like watching a poor performance on video tape, there may also be portions of our lives that we would rather not face: our hidden motives, pride, selfishness, and other sins that we would rather keep covered and in the dark.

David wrote, "Search me, O God, and know my heart; test me and know my anxious thoughts. See if there is any offensive way in me, and lead me in the way everlasting," (Psalm 139:23-24).

It is foolishness to think that we can hide anything from God's eyes! It is equally foolish to intentionally close off areas of our lives from examination when we know that what's inside is keeping us separated from God.

God gave us a gift in His Word. God's Word is a guide, "a lamp to my feet," (Psalm 119:105). As we dig deeper into His Word, it guides our steps and also reveals our heart. Using God's Word to truly examine our life can be painful. It seems that as soon as we strip back one layer, we expose additional layers of sin that we didn't even know we had.

If we desire to improve our performance in life, we must be determined to live a life that brings our Master Coach glory and honor in all we do. We must be willing to open our lives to allow His Spirit to search us and wash us with His Word. We must be willing to be totally committed. We must strive for holiness. We must live a self-examined life.

PERFORMANCE PRINCIPLE 33

TEAMMATES

One of the greatest things about athletics is the people you work and train with every day. That's why so many professional athletes have a hard time finally retiring because they realize that they will miss the camaraderie of teammates and coaches more than the game itself.

Over the years, I have competed with or coached thousands of athletes. During that time many strong bonds and ties were developed. What I always hated most about coaching, was that the friends I learned to love and trust through the battles and challenges of athletic competition would continually move on, either to better coaching situations or to graduation. It is always sad to see them go, knowing that life would never be the same without them. What is so special about sport is the relationships you build. There is something special about the dream, the sweat, the pain, and the drive to the goal that bonds athletes and coaches together. You come to realize that it is impossible to do it alone in sport; you really do need someone at your side.

I was blessed to have the best coaching friend ever in Mike Imhoff. He was a gift from God. Mike played football at Michigan State in the mid-70s. He was a tremendous athlete. We hit it off the very day we met as rookie coaches at Michigan Tech. That year he ate every meal in our home and became part of our family. Mike was there for all my kid's birthdays. We hunted and got lost in the woods. We put up lopsided Christmas trees.

We watched game film until 2:30 in the morning. We rejoiced in the wins, and hurt in the losses. We shared a tearful hug as he left for a coaching job at Montana State. Years passed. When there was a chance to coach together again, I moved my family from Upper Michigan to Florida to be with him.

We laughed, joked and cried together. We pushed each other. We cut school to golf and fish together. We argued and fought over game plans and play calling. We sat up late into the night sharing our failures, and talked about our dreams. We talked about God and His love, and how to have a personal relationship with Him.

I decided I wanted to coach in college again, and so I moved my family to Minnesota. Mike and I would talk for hours on the phone. The last time I spoke with him, we talked about coaching together again. It was something we both wanted to do. Days later in January 1996, God took Mike home. Oh, Lord I miss him!

God never intended us to go into battle alone. He knew we would need someone to share the burden and provide necessary encouragement during the tough times. While He always cares for us and our burdens, His Word also directs us to draw upon the strength of others for daily encouragement: "encourage on another daily, as long as it is called Today, so that none of you may be hardened by sin's deceitfulness," (Hebrews 3:13).

Immediately after creating the first man, God said, "It is not good for man to be alone," (Genesis 2:18). We were created to be people who need one another. King Solomon learned this wise lesson, "Two are better than one…if one falls down, his friend can help him up," (Ecclesiastes 4:9-10). And when Jesus sent out the seventy-two messengers to proclaim that the Kingdom of God is near, He "sent them two by two," (Luke 10:1). Difficult tasks require mutual support and encouragement.

As we travel down God's path, let's listen to His counsel and not walk alone. Let's entrust our lives to our heavenly Father and seek other believers who will encourage us to remain in His presence and aligned with His perfect will. Let's pray that God would bless us with an abundance of spiritual teammates along the way. We really do need each other.

PERFORMANCE PRINCIPLE 34

THE GREATEST OF ALL DAYS

Every summer there are induction ceremonies to both the Major League Baseball and the Pro Football Hall of Fame. Crowds of people travel to the Football Hall of Fame in Canton, Ohio, or to the Baseball Hall of Fame in Cooperstown, New York, to see the ceremonies, to catch a glimpse of the greats from the past, and maybe just shake a hand or capture an autograph from one of these living legends.

There always is an air of excitement for the inductees. They are in awe to be part of the Hall of Fame. They are filled with gratitude to those who helped them along the way: parents, coaches, and teammates; and they struggle to fight back the tears of thankfulness for having such a great opportunity. The chance to play a game and play it well, to be honored by one's peers, and to be given the highest honor in sports makes this a great day in their lives.

As athletes and coaches, we all dream about excelling. We all hope that one day we will be honored for our efforts and achievements. How wonderful it would be to stand among the all-time greats and be a part of that team.

For the Christian athlete and coach, we are assured that one day we will be honored. How exciting it will be when Jesus greets us at the banquet hall, shakes our hand, gives us a big hug, and says, "Well done my good and faithful friend." He then turns to His Father and His angels and says, "Yes, Father, I know him. He belongs here with us," (Revelation 3:5). We are not given a bust or a plaque, but awarded a crown of life (Revelation 2:10).

All the greats will be there: Abel, Noah, Abraham, Isaac, Jacob, Joseph, Moses, "Gideon, Barak, Samson, Jephthah, David, Samuel, and all the prophets...these people overthrew kingdoms, ruled with justice, and received what God had promised them. They shut the mouths of lions, quenched the flames of fire, and escaped death by the edge of the sword. Their weakness was turned to strength. They became strong in battle and put whole armies to flight. Women received their love ones back again from death. But others trusted God and were tortured, preferring to die rather than turn from God and be free. They placed their hope in the resurrection to a better life. Some were mocked, and their backs were cut open with whips. Others were chained in dungeons. Some died by stoning, and some were sawed in half; others were killed with the sword. Some went in skins of sheep and goats, hungry and oppressed and mistreated," (Hebrews 11;32-37, NLT). It will be an incredible gathering of the faithful!

This Heavenly Hall of Fame induction will be beyond all comprehension. The press release concerning the ceremony states that: "No eye has seen, no ear has heard, no mind has conceived what God has prepared for those who love him," (1 Corinthians 2:10). This will be the greatest of all days. I pray that you will be there too!

PERFORMANCE PRINCIPLE 35

WHOM DO YOU BELIEVE?

Rocky Bleier was not very big or very fast, but he was an incredibly determined athlete when the Pittsburgh Steelers picked him in the 1968 NFL draft. Before he could prove himself as a rookie fullback, Bleier was drafted again—this time for combat duty in Vietnam with the United States Army.

Crippled by enemy rifle fire and grenade wounds in both legs, Bleier faced his biggest challenge. One afternoon in the army hospital, doctor after doctor came in to give the final verdict. "Rocky, you won't play again—it is impossible." He could barely walk, he certainly couldn't run. To ever play professional football again seemed almost impossible.

However, Rocky Bleier did not listen to his doctor's reports. Rocky believed that if he trained hard enough he could make it all the way to the Steelers. Rocky trained like a madman, pushing his body physically and mentally to the max. Make it back Rocky did! Bleier enjoyed a twelve-year career with Pittsburgh. He became one of the Steelers' top ground-gainers, passed the 1,000 yard rushing mark for one season, and contributed to four Super Bowl Championships.

What would life had been like for Rocky Bleier if he had believed his doctors?

Sadly, too many people let the negativity of this world rob them of God's best. They say, "I can't go to college, nobody in my family ever has!" or "I can't make the varsity team; I'm just not good enough!" or "I'm just not big enough or strong enough to make it to that level of competition." They give up hope and quit before receiving what God promised.

This is something you need to realize: God is bigger than any problem or adversity you face! To realize God's promises, we must obey His Word. "Keep on asking, and you will be given what you ask for. Keep on looking, and you will find. Keep on knocking, and the door will be opened," (Luke 11:9, NLT).

God also promises, "For I know the plans I have for you,' says the LORD. 'They are plans for good and not disaster, to give you a future and a hope," (Jeremiah 29:11, NLT).

So then, whom are you going to believe—the defeating words of your friends, parents, coaches, doctors, fans, and the media—or God's words of life?

May God bless you as you stand in faith. Believe in all His wonderful promises; they are for you!

PERFORMANCE PRINCIPLE 36

SACRIFICE = SUCCESS

Ted Williams is considered by many as the greatest hitter that ever played the game of baseball. Williams was the last major league ball player to hit over .400 and left the game with a lifetime batting average of .344 and 521 home runs—this in spite of the fact that he sacrificed the prime of his career to service in the Marine Air Corp in both World War II and in the Korean War.

Ted Williams did not achieve this success because he was a "natural." Williams worked at developing his craft. He studied hitting as if it were a science. He studied and did his homework on every pitcher in the American League. According to his roommate, while traveling on road trips, Ted would swing rolled up newspaper, pillows, anything to practice his swing during the middle of the night.

Ted Williams paid a price to be the best hitter in the game. In spring training each year, Williams spent so much time with a bat in his hands that they would blister, then bleed. By the time the regular season would start his hands would be callused and ready for the demands of the season. Now ready, a bat in the hands of Ted Williams was a weapon of destruction—against every pitcher in the league.

Time after time, success comes down to sacrifice—the willingness to pay the price. Without the conviction that the cause is worth the price, the battle will never be won, and success will never be realized. There must be commitment.

Jesus taught his disciples and the crowds that followed Him, "If any of you wants to be my follower,' he told them, 'you must put aside your selfish ambition, shoulder your cross, and follow me. If you try to keep your life for yourself, you will lose it. But if you give up your life for my sake and for the sake of the Good News, you will find true life," (Mark 8:34-35, NLT).

Jesus used the image of carrying a cross to illustrate the ultimate submission and sacrifice required of His followers. He was not against pleasure, nor is He saying that we should seek pain needlessly. Jesus was talking about the heroic effort needed to follow him moment by moment, to do His will even when the work is difficult and the future looks tough.

Jesus wants us to choose to follow Him rather than to choose to lead a life of sin and self-satisfaction—and that takes commitment. It is through commitment to Christ that we know what it means to live abundantly now and have eternal life. That is true and lasting success—a sacrifice truly worth the price.

PERFORMANCE PRINCIPLE 37

THE GRIND MATCH

Steve Fraser is the National Coach for Greco-Roman wrestling in the United States. Steve is an intense, fierce competitor, who was an Olympic champion as an athlete. In his training plan, he institutes what he calls "the grind match." The grind match is the most brutal, intense training method I know of. It is a continuous wrestling match that last one to two hours in length! It is live wrestling activity where the final score is not as important as some of the other benefits a wrestler can gain from the exercise.

What are the rules? Coach Fraser says it is pretty simple. Keep wrestling, nonstop, for the entire, predetermined time. Absolutely no stopping is allowed. No sitting on the sidelines for a minute to catch your breath. No going to the drinking fountain two or three times for a water break. No lengthy tying of your shoes or adjusting your shorts. Wrestling is continuous on the feet and on the mat. The walls, if they are padded, are inbounds! Coach Fraser says one of the greatest benefits is that you will learn to keep moving, no matter what, and most of all, you will learn how to break your opponent's will to fight.

Going hard for an hour in a "grind match" is brutal. It is mentally and physically exhausting to say the least.

Coach Fraser's grind matches remind me that we, too, are in a daily grind match. God has put us there for a specific training purpose. The battle we are in is not a short drill match, but a grind match of eternal consequences. There is not time to catch five, gulp down some Gatorade, and catch your breath. We are in the midst of the battle, a spiritual war where everything—from the enemy's perspective—is inbounds and in play. He has one purpose, to destroy you.

Unless you have a solid foundation (know Jesus as Lord and Savior), have the technical knowledge (know God's Word) and have an overall base of conditioning (prayer time), you will not be able to go the distance. Otherwise the enemy opponent (Satan) will pound on you and break your will.

The only successful individuals are those who understand the terms of engagement (see Ephesians 6:10-18); they are the only ones who can battle all the way through the night, in blood and sweat, scraping, pummeling, and fighting until they receive the blessing (Genesis 32:22-32).

The Master Coach puts us in a grind match so that we are continually molded and toughened up. To be a team member of His squad, you need to know firsthand the truth about sacrifice and suffering. You can't just watch it on a video or read about it in the playbook, you need to experience it for yourself. Remember only those who can go the distance will be rewarded!

How about you? Are you tough enough to go the distance?

PERFORMANCE PRINCIPLE 38

ON FIRE

For some athletes, their sport is a passion. They pursue victory with a full measure of their heart and soul. They pour themselves out, they give everything they have in their training. They spend themselves entirely in their strength workouts, in their aerobic conditioning, and tactical preparation. They stick to their diet, and they get their rest. They come early to practice, and they are the last to leave. They have a fire that burns deep in their heart.

An athlete on fire in this way is a special breed. These are the ones who flat out love to compete and win. They compete for the love of the sport, and because they love it, they want to be the best at it. They are not in it for the awards, rather they work for the intrinsic rewards of pushing themselves to the next level.

There are many more athletes who are lukewarm—only a few are actually on fire. And lukewarm athletes seldom realize they are lukewarm; in fact, most of them are likely pretty satisfied. They are probably thinking that they are on the right track, that everything is just fine.

Jesus had some harsh words for those who are lukewarm: "So, because you are lukewarm—neither hot nor cold—I am about to spit you out of my mouth," (Revelations 3:16).

Luke warm athletes are everywhere; our courts, fields, pools, and mats are full of them. Why? Because the object of their passion are either vain or superficial. Theodore Roosevelt once said:

> The credit belongs to the man who is actually in the arena; whose face is marred by dust and sweat and blood; who strives valiantly; who errs and comes short again and again; who knows the great enthusiasms, the great devotions and spends himself in a worthy cause. Who at the best, knows the triumph of high achievement; and who, at the worst, if he fails, at least fails while daring greatly.

This type of athlete for whom coaches search, and this is the kind of athlete upon whom God smiles. In Colossians 3:23 it is written, "Whatever you do, work at it with all your heart..." It pleases God when we put all of our heart into significant pursuits. But God also looks at our motives. The second part of the verse, along with verse 24 adds, "work at it with all your heart, as working for the Lord, not for men, since you know that you will receive an inheritance from the Lord as a reward. It is the Lord Christ you are serving" (Colossians 3:23-24).

God is looking for an athlete who's heart is on fire for Him—someone who will rise early, who schedules a special time each day to be just with Him, just because they love Him. King David wrote, "his delight is in the law of the LORD, and on his law [i.e. God's Word, the Bible], he meditates day and night. He is like a tree planted by streams of water, which yields its fruit in season and whose leaf does not wither. Whatever he does prospers" (Psalm 1:3).

This is not a picture of a lukewarm person. It is a portrait of a person who is aflame with the love of God—a person who is hot on God's trail. God is looking for those who will go after Him nonstop, with the same intensity with which they might compete and train for sport.

Strength will fade, zeal will wither, but the person who yearns for God with all their heart, day and night delighting in and meditating on His Word, that person will prosper in everything he does. He will be a well-watered tree growing strong and vibrant, able to withstand long droughts and formidable adversity. That hot, burning fire for the Lord—is it in you?

PERFORMANCE PRINCIPLE 39

LISTEN UP!

I have been blessed to coach in some big, important venues during my coaching career: world championships, Pan American championships, and national championships. Some of the greatest challenges I have faced were simply being able to communicate with my athletes during the heat of the battle.

The loud cheering from the crowd, the competing voices shouting advice, and the bright lights can create a barrier between the coach and the athlete when communication—*when coaching can become so important.* Sometimes it has been so loud that you could not even hear yourself scream.

One time, coming off the mat after a match, I put my arm around my athlete, bent over and congratulated her on her performance, and shouted into her ear, “Could you even hear me out there?” She responded, “You’re the only voice I heard.” My athletes and I spend a lot of time together—they know my voice.

Jesus said, “My sheep listen to my voice; I know them, and they follow me” (John 10:27).

How often do we set aside time to listen to the voice of our heavenly Father? If we only occasionally listen, will we even recognize His voice when He calls? We must not wait until the crisis of the battle. If we haven’t learned to filter out the competing noise of the blaring worldly chaos, God’s call will be lost in the noise and confusion of the crowd.

We must spend time away from the noise where we can be

alone with God and learn to recognize His voice. We must establish times to be quiet, to read His Word, and to talk with Him in prayer. Spending time in the Word of God can set us apart from the distractions of the world. By meditating on His truth and praying for understanding, we can refine our spiritual filter. When we enter the battle, there may be thousands of competing voices, but a properly tuned filter will allow only a single voice to pass.

Let's develop the discipline of listening along with the spiritual skill to filter the voices of the crowd to the singular voice of our Lord. Our faith will be enough to respond—strong enough to take the step, but first we must have the ability to hear the call. It is important that we begin to "listen up!"

PERFORMANCE PRINCIPLE 40

GETTING BACK INTO THE GAME

Getting back into the game following an injury or and extended layoff is a tough challenge for any athlete. In fact, the National Football League and Major League Baseball give awards to the "Comeback Player of the Year."

The challenges are twofold. First, following an injury and possible surgery, the athlete needs to rehab. The rehabilitation process can be brutal. I have seen tough guys cry during assisted stretching following knee surgery, and the sheer frustration of bench pressing five-pound dumbbells after reconstructive shoulder surgery can be agonizing. It takes perseverance and discipline to work through this stage.

Then there are the psychological challenges. The athlete's primary fear is injuring himself again. This is followed by the fear of diminished ability—"Will I be able to do what I used to do?" The speed, strength, timing, endurance, and faith might not be there for him yet. The athlete needs to concentrate on the task, take baby steps, focus on the overall fundamentals of the sport, and see the daily progress in overcoming the frustration of not being 100 percent healthy yet. The bottom line is that it takes time and a lot of hard work and discipline to get back into the game.

I received an E-mail from a former athlete who is serving as a missionary in Mexico for a year. She just returned to Guadalajara after a holiday back at home:

"Dear Coach!! Things are going well for me—just different than before. I am having a little bit of a problem getting back into it. I mean, I still love it here—and I love what I do—I am just having a problem getting my heart back into it. So please pray for me!"

Sometimes as Christians we have a tough time getting back into the game with God. We have fallen away, backslid, or are just having a problem with getting back to the level of spirituality we once knew. The struggle and the frustration is finding how to get back into the "spiritual zone" that we once enjoyed.

The "spiritual zone" is realized only by being intimate with God. It takes time and effort to reach the zone; it begins with going back to the fundamentals.

The fundamentals start with spending quality time with Him. Take time to read His Word in a version of the Bible that speaks to you the best. I like the clarity and simplicity of *The Message.* Reading His Word helps you understand the heart of God. Next, take the time to meditate on what you just read. Chew on those verses. Ask, "how does it apply to me today?" Then you need to take the time to pray, to speak to God. Speak to Him from your heart, like you would do with your best and most trusted friend. He longs to hear from you.

Finally, it takes forgiveness and repentance. We need to forgive those who hurt us, and seek forgiveness of those whom we have sinned against, then actively turn away from sin. Getting back into the game takes a lot of hard work and discipline.

Fundamentals must be practiced each day, and when done every day they form a habit. This habit then becomes a ritual that keeps you in the zone. If you are struggling with your sport or with the Lord, get back to the fundamentals—it is the basic skills that get you back into the game—and help you to perform like a champion.

PERFORMANCE PRINCIPLE 41

WEAR THE COLORS WITH PRIDE

Not long ago I was in Phoenix for important international wrestling competition. We didn't have the best travel plans. Our itinerary kept us laid over in Phoenix for 23 hours after the competition of our event. Not wanting to just sit around the hotel all day, I made arrangements to go with James Johnson, a former U.S. World Greco-Roman wrestling team member to attend services at the Good Samaritan Church, just a couple of blocks from the Arizona State University campus.

As I left my room that morning and walked down to the hotel lobby to meet J.J., I was shocked to find that the hotel was filled with Dallas Cowboy fans. It was like ants at a picnic in the desert. Cowboy fans moved in and out of the hotel in waves of silver and blue.

I saw literally hundreds of Emmit Smith jerseys, not to mention the T-shirts and assorted polo shirts that proclaimed they were loyal fans of "America's Team." The fans wore Cowboy hats, Cowboy sunglasses, toted Cowboy coolers, carried Cowboy seat cushions, and even had Cowboy pillows. I witnessed fathers holding their infant sons decked out in miniature Cowboy uniforms, kids playing catch in the hotel parking lot with their Cowboy footballs, and full-grown men with their heads painted to look like a Cowboy football helmet.

You could not ignore their love, their passion, and their commitment to their team. They wore the colors with pride, and some even sported tattoos declaring a more than permanent brand of loyalty.

All this just for a football game.

It stuck me as odd how we will travel hundred of miles, spend thousand of dollars, wear clothes and accessories that proclaim our loyalties, and perhaps even tattoo our flesh to show our commitment; yet when it comes to Christ we often bite our tongue and sit silent about our faith. Shouldn't it really be different?

Jesus put it this way, "You're here to be light, bringing out the God-colors in the world. God is not a secret to be kept. We're going public with this, as public as a city on a hill. If I make you light-bearers, you don't think I'm going to hide you under a bucket, do you? I'm putting you on a light stand. Now that I've put you there on a hilltop, on a light stand—shine!" (Matthew 5:14-16, THE MESSAGE)

Shine—that is what Christ wants from you! You can't shine on your own; it is Christ who shines through you as you draw closer and nearer to Him. The Bible tells it this way: "the Word was God," and "the Word was light," and that "Christ is the Light of the world." Thus, the light that shines through you becomes of greater illumination when you hunger and thirst for more of the Word—more of God.

When Christ died on the cross, His sacrificial death became an offer to receive a free gift of salvation. Through His loving gift, He offers to wash us clean of sin. "Though your sins are like scarlet, they shall be as white as snow; though they are red as crimson, they shall be like wool" (Isaiah 1:18). God is offering us the opportunity to wear a new color as part of His team.

Today, let's start wearing our new team colors with pride. We need to show the world whose team we are on. We can't be afraid to wear them, or to show off the light. We must feel the need to recruit others to the team by just simply sharing the love, the hope, the peace, the truth, and the salvation we have found in Christ. No matter what you do, no matter where you are, let your light shine on!

PERFORMANCE PRINCIPLE 42

NO BRAG, JUST FACT

Ricky Henderson is a tremendously talented major league baseball player. In 25 seasons in the big leagues, Henderson was able to capture a number of all-time baseball records. Henderson holds the major league record for the most walks and for the most stolen bases in a career. He also has been honored with a selection to the All-Star Game on numerous occasions, a Golden Glove, the Silver Shoe, and has been named the American League's Most Valuable Player.

Ricky also holds the record for the most home runs for a player leading off. He holds the major league record for the most stolen bases in a season, the most years with 50 or more stolen bases, and the most consecutive years with 50 or more stolen bases. And Henderson has rapped out more than 3,000 hits in his career joining an elite list of baseball's greatest players.

When Ricky broke Lou Brock's all-time stolen-base record, Lou Brock was there to present Ricky the base with which he broke the record in honor of the great feat. Lou was gracious with his words in honoring the new record holder. Ricky accepted the base, raising it over his head and said, "I am now the greatest of all time!"

Another former base-stealing great, Ty Cobb once said, "It ain't bragging if you can back it up." In the past we have heard similar quotes from other athletes. Muhammad Ali always said, "I am the greatest!"

It is an interesting concept that God favors humility over bragging. James writes, "As it is, you boast and brag. All such boasting is evil" (James 4:16). And the apostle John writes, "For everything in the world—the cravings of sinful man, the lust of his eyes and the boasting of what he has and does—comes not from the Father but from the world" (1 John 2:16).

Watching the Little League World Series I have noted sadly these 10-14 year old athletes are following the model set for them by Ricky Henderson. What a shame! It is not Ricky, the Babe, or Ty we need to follow, but Joseph, the son of Jacob and Rachel in the Old Testament.

The Pharaoh of Egypt was seeking answers in regard to the meaning of the strange dreams he had been having. He asked many different people to help him, but no one came forward except a prisoner in his jail. Joseph sent word from his cell that he was willing to help. "Pharaoh said to Joseph, 'I had a dream, and no one can interpret it. But I have heard it said of you that when you hear a dream you can interpret it.'

'I cannot do it,' Joseph replied to Pharaoh, 'but God will give Pharaoh the answer he desires" (Genesis 41:16).

Joseph could have said, "Yes, I have a gift of interpretation. I will help you." Or Joseph could have said, "O Pharaoh, I will interpret your dream if you let me out of prison." Since the dreams were troubling Pharaoh, he probably would have cut a deal with Joseph. However, the Bible seems to indicate that Joseph's primary objective was to use his gift to bring glory to God.

Thinking about Joseph as a role model for us, the primary objective for us as Christian athletes and coaches is to use our skills and abilities to bring glory to God. The real danger we face is to accept the praise from teammates, coaches, the media, fans, etc., without acknowledging God as the One who provides the skills and abilities to do the work.

So just how can I glorify God? This is a challenge, but Paul gives us a coaching tip we can use. "Do nothing out of selfish ambition or vain conceit, but in humility consider others better than yourselves. Each of you should look not only to your own interests, but also to the interests of others" (Philippians 2:3-4). Focusing on yourself is an act of pride, taking your eyes off yourself and looking to the needs of others is an act of humility. Consider the true example, which is the life of Christ (Philippians 2:5-9).

Jesus taught in Matthew 5:16, "Let your light shine before men, that they may see your good deeds and praise your Father in heaven." As Christ's love and light reflect off of us, we too must reflect back all the praise and glory to the King saying, "It is He—not I!" No brag, just fact!

PERFORMANCE PRINCIPLE 43

RECEIVE THE GIFT

One thing is sure in sport: athletes work extremely hard to make it to the top. The long hours, the sacrifice, the pain; they all pay the price just to taste the sweetness of victory. Too often in sport, the sweetness is replaced with the taste of bitterness.

Consider the 2002 Winter Olympics when Russian figure skaters Yelena Bereezhnaya and Anton Sikharulidze were awarded the Gold medal after performing a less-than-perfect routine while Canadians Jamie Sale and David Pelletier were awarded a second place finish after a flawless performance in the same competition.

Consider 2001 World Series hero Luis Gonzales who won the Series for the Diamondbacks with a seventh game, bottom-of-the-ninth-inning hit. A year later, in the final weeks of the 2002 season, Gonzales tore up his shoulder with the Diamond-backs looking to repeat.

Consider NFL All-Pro and NFC Most Valuable Player, Kurt Warner, of the St. Louis Rams. He broke his pinky finger in the fourth game of the 2002 season and was out for 8-10 weeks. While he is recovering, the Rams' title hopes were dashed.

Consider freestyle wrestler Chris Bono. Bono has been knocking at the door for years behind his long time rival. In 2002, Bono won a spot on the US World Team, but because of politics and the danger of terrorism, the US team does not trav-el to Iran to compete in the world championships. Bono and his teammates sit at home and wonder what might have been.

Consider high school senior football captain Chris Reese. He punished his body in the weight room and endured intense off-season conditioning to be ready for his senior season. The six-foot, 215-pound fullback was averaging four yards a carry, and was an emotional leader on his team. In the fifth game of the season, on a routine block, his knee pops and he goes down with an ACL injury. The season and the dream are over.

The unexpected arrival of adversity faces all of us. Its presence comes in many shapes and forms. In sports it goes by many names: injury or sickness, slumps, poor officiating, world politics, adverse weather, difficult teammates, etc.—the list goes on. Jesus said, "For he gives his sunlight to both the evil and the good, and he sends rain on the just and on the unjust, too" (Matthew 5:45, NLT). Adversity happens to all of us—and it really ought not to come as a surprise. Despite knowing this, my son Chris and my wife and I were stunned and in tears.

It is human nature to respond to adversity with tears, anger, and the question, "Why me?" Sometimes life is seemingly so unfair!

Stop and consider the Old Testament character Job for a moment. Here was an upright and righteous man. God said it was so, that his ways were blameless. When Satan struck Job with a terrible case of boils from head to toe, he maintained a proper attitude concerning his situation. Even when Job's wife encouraged him to curse God for this tribulation, Job stood firm. "Should we accept only good things from the hand of God and never anything bad?" (Job 2:10, NLT).

Job's principles were tested. During the course of his suffering, he raised one of the central questions with which all Christians must eventually wrestle. Is our relationship with God conditional or complete—regardless of the pain, injury, setback, or injustice?

Paul writes to the Romans on this very subject, "And we know that God causes everything to work together for the good of those who love God and are called according to his purpose for them" (Romans 8:28, NLT). So no matter how bad things look right now, God has a plan for the outcome to be good. He also has a plan and purpose for you. "They are plans for good and not for disaster, to give you a future and a hope" (Jeremiah 29:11, NLT).

We need to learn to accept adversity as a gift from God. The gift has a purpose, as it is intended to draw the recipient into a deeper relationship with Him and to increase one's level of commitment. How we respond to this invitation from God to get closer to Him in the midst of our trouble and anguish will determine whether or not we will understand that it is truly a loving gift rather than a weapon to harm us. If we curse God for this gift, we miss out on deeper blessings and closer communion with Him. What a blessing it is to draw nearer to God, who gave up His only Son for each of us! Receive the gift openly and with confidence. Run to the giver!

PERFORMANCE PRINCIPLE 44

BEING IN THE RIGHT PLACE

Tony Gonzalez is a talented athlete. He plays for the Kansas City Chiefs in the National Football League as a tight end. Gonzalez's skills are so good on the football field he was recognized with All-Pro honors. But that is not all Gonzalez can do. In college, he also played basketball at the University of California. During his collegiate days, Tony averaged 6.4 points and 4.3 rebounds a game as a forward.

When most pro football players are relaxing before the start of training camp, Tony Gonzalez is trying out for the Miami Heat of the National Basketball Association. He said he will not give up football, but he is also serious about playing for the Heat.

"I had a pretty good camp," said Gonzalez. "I did what I wanted to do out here. These guys gave me a chance, and hopefully I was able to come out here and prove that I could do it."

Gonzalez was impressive in the Heat's summer league camp. "He would have made our team if he was just another guy, so why would you cut him just because he's a football player?" assistant coach Stan Van Gundy said. "He earned his way, plain and simple."

So what should Tony Gonzalez do? What would you do? Football? Basketball? Or do both?

If we keep our life under the will and authority of God, we are going to be in the right place, doing the right thing. When you are right with God he will point the way for you. You won't have to wonder if you are doing the right thing—you will have inner assurance. Too often our worldly plans and desires are pulling us away from what God wants us to do. Like a pendulum, we swing closer to, and then farther away from His plan for us. We are all go through times like this.

But if we decide to draw closer to God, then He draws closer to us (James 4:8). A clear view of God gives a clear picture of our lives as well, and then we are better able to see God's direction for future decisions. Road maps are easily read close up, but did you ever try to read one from across the room? The Word of God is the road map of life up close. Surround yourself with the things of God. The music you listen to, the company you keep, the books you read, and the TV shows you watch also determine your proximity to God.

The world has so many things that pull and tug at us. "Find satisfaction here, get glory over there." As athletes and coaches we are supposed to be self-confident and full of our own strength. All around the world, athletes and coaches are looked at as gods! We are told that we should have this salary, this job, this toy, and this honor. This all feeds into believing that we can do it on our own, that our plans are sufficient, and that we deserve it. Led astray, we go off and make our own plans without God's input.

The truth is, it is more important to be Biblically correct, than political correct in the decisions we make. Our lives are completely dependent upon the grace, mercy and power of God. We cannot be proud and boast of future plans and accomplishments. We must live day-by-day, seeking His will and making plans as He leads us. Then knowing His will, we must commit ourselves to do it—then we will not only be in the right place—but, the perfect place.

PERFORMANCE PRINCIPLE 45

GO TO PRACTICE

Webster defines practice as: "to perform or work repeatedly so as to become proficient; to train by repeated exercises; to do or perform often, customarily, or habitually."

Champions are recognized in the arena, but they are made in practice through the refining of technique, the adaptation of strategy, the agony of conditioning, and by the discipline of building strength. Champions are not born, they are created in the process of continued, long-term effort, saturated with discipline, through repetition.

For practice to be effective, discipline is required. Being disciplined in your life is not easy, there is temptation daily to slack off, not give your best, and to "save yourself" for conditioning at the end of practice. Yes, there are days when you feel tired, are sick, have too much homework to do, or even when problems of the world penetrate your life those are the days when you really would like to skip practice. In these situations it is your discipline, your mental toughness that takes over and can carry you through and keep you on the right path.

Jesus said to His disciples, "Keep alert and pray. Otherwise temptation will overpower you. For the spirit is willing, but how weak the body is!" (Matthew 26:41, NLT).

Jesus, the Master Coach, is instructing us that we need to attend to His practice sessions to become spiritually tough and disciplined enough to overcome the temptations and distractions of life. He calls us to promise Him and ourselves to carve out time in our hectic lifestyle to attend to the practice of prayer, fasting, service, and intense study and meditation on His playbook, the Bible.

Attending practice sessions with God not only polishes our character and develops wisdom in our lives, it delivers us up to the next level of godly obedience, builds upon our personal relationship with Christ, and it continues to build our spiritual toughness to defeat the relentless temptations of the enemy.

If you plan on getting into the game and enjoying the taste of victory, then go to practice every day.

PERFORMANCE PRINCIPLE 46

WHERE IS YOUR CONFIDENCE?

In ancient Greece there was a champion that stood above all the rest as a hero in the world of sport. Milo of Crotona was Olympic champion six times in his 24 year long athletic career—and champion of the Pythian Games five times, champion of the Nemean Games nine times, and champion of the Isthmian Games ten times, not to mention countless championships of lesser importance.

Ancient historian Pausanius wrote about some of Milo's fascinating qualities as an athlete. When holding something in his hand, whether a stone or fruit; no one could make him drop it. His grasp was so steady that not a single drop would fall from ripe fruit while it was in his hand. He was so steady on his feet that even when standing on an oiled discus, no one could tip him off balance, not even move him. Milo could run around the stadium carrying a four year-old bull. He was so strong that he could carry his own statue.

According to another writer, Stabon, while Milo was attending a meeting of Pythagoreans, a supporting column to the meeting place began to crumble. Milo supported the roof with his own body until everyone got safely out from under the roof.

Legend has it that this outstanding athlete, second to none, was actually killed by the betrayal of his own self-confidence. Milo wanted to split a tree in two with his own hands, but his hands got caught between two pieces of the tree. He could not free himself, and at the end he was devoured by wolves.

In Genesis chapter 32, the Bible speaks of the preparation of Jacob to face his older brother Esau. Esau had vowed to kill Jacob because of stealing his birthright through deception and manipulation. Jacob had his back against the wall. Until this point in his life, Jacob was a self-made man. It seemed as if Jacob really did not need God because he had been able to use his wits and ingenuity to solve all the issues of his life.

One night, a "Man" started wrestling with Jacob. Many scholars think that the "Man" was God. Even before Jacob was born, God had placed His blessing on him. Yet, Jacob spent most of his time getting the most out of life, running on his own confidence. At this point, Jacob stood face-to-face with God in a wrestling match. He was no match for God!

Jacob appeared to be the type of person who thought that he could think his way out of any situation. In a sense, God had blessed him with wit and ingenuity. It was through the wrestling match that God wanted to show Jacob that placing his confidence in Him was much better than placing in his own human abilities.

The apostle Paul also supports this principle in his letter to the Philippians. After presenting an impressive resume of his accomplishments, Paul goes on to say, "I consider everything a loss compared to the surpassing greatness of knowing Christ Jesus my Lord, for whose sake I have lost all things. I consider them rubbish, that I may gain Christ and be found in him" (Philippians 3:8-9). King David agreed, "Some trust in chariots and some in horses, but we trust in the name of the LORD our God" (Psalm 20:7).

For Jacob, it seemed that his confidence stemmed from his ingenuity and cunning, but God wanted his confidence to come directly from Him. Perhaps God's desire for you is to realize that your confidence should not come from performance incentives, medals, trophies, titles and championships, honors in the media, job advancement, big contracts, education, moral conduct, or any other human effort. We need to learn to trust God, and allow Him to teach us to place all of our confidence in Him—and not on our natural abilities. Only then will we find true success.

PERFORMANCE PRINCIPLE 47

TOUGH UNDER PRESSURE

The 1999 National Football League season was a time of trial and adversity for Tampa Bay Buccaneer quarterback Trent Dilfer. The Bucs were slated to have a fine season. As they faltered near midseason, Dilfer took the brunt of the heat from the media and the hometown fans. Shortly thereafter he was replaced by Shawn King and delegated to the backup role at quarterback.

The Bucs then surged into the postseason eventually losing to the St. Louis Rams in the NFC Championship game. After the season, Dilfer was deemed expendable and dealt to the Baltimore Ravens as a backup quarterback. Adversity had sacked Trent Dilfer for what seemed like a big loss.

King Solomon wrote that, "If you fail under pressure, your strength is not very great" (Proverbs 24:10, NLT).

Many athletes would have been bitter and would have crumbled, but not Dilfer. "My only expectation was to get better," he said. "To develop the talent that God has given me. To be the best teammate I could be. Whatever that role was. Every week you face a new challenge, and you just have to embrace them."

Times of trouble and adversity can be useful. Difficult situations can show you who you really are—what kind of character you have developed. In addition, they can help you grow stronger. When Jeremiah questioned God because of the trouble he faced, God asked how he ever expected to face big challenges if the little ones tired him out (Jeremiah 12:5).

"You can't go running from adversity," says Trent Dilfer. "You have to let it hit you straight in the face. You have to allow God to build character in you."

Don't complain about your problems. The challenges you face today are training you to be strong for the difficult situations you will face in the future. Just ask Super Bowl XXXIV champion quarterback, Trent Dilfer. Stay tough under pressure.

PERFORMANCE PRINCIPLE 48

NO LIMITS

A few years ago I took a challenge from my college wrestlers to compete in the Master's World Championships in freestyle wrestling. I had no preconceived notion on the results—I just wanted to compete again. I trained hard for a number of months leading up to the event, and the more I trained, the more the competitive juices flowed within me. When I arrived in Toronto, I sized up my competition at weigh-ins. I decided that there was a possibility of winning a medal.

I realized that I had probably trained harder than any of my competition. As a collegiate wrestling coach, I had the advantage of wrestling every day with my team members. Once I saw the draw, I felt that my first impression at the weigh-ins had been conservative. *I had a pretty good chance of bringing home a medal, and it wouldn't matter at all whether it was gold, silver or bronze.*

On Friday afternoon, when I defeated my opponent in the semifinals, I clinched my goal of winning a medal. That night I slept soundly, content in reaching my goal. The next day when I arrived at the venue there was not the normal greeting of "butterflies" in my stomach. I was not at all nervous as I stepped onto the mat to meet my Canadian opponent for the gold medal. Satisfied that I had reached my goal, I got whipped by my adversary, and even broke my hand in the process!

Goals and goal setting is all important to the athlete. But sometimes, as I learned in Toronto, through goal setting we place artificial limitations or restrictions on what we think we can accomplish.

There is a story in 2 Kings about a widow who came to the prophet Elisha for help with her finances. Creditors had threatened to take her two boys as slaves in exchange for payment of the debt. The women told Elisha that all she had left was a little bit of oil, but he told her how to miraculously multiply what she has so she could pay off her bills.

"Go around and ask all your neighbors for empty jars. Don't ask for just a few. Then go inside and shut the door behind you and your sons. Pour oil into all the jars, and as each is filled, put it to one side" (2 Kings 4:3).

The woman gathered empty jars and began to fill them each with the oil from her one small jar. She continued to fill the jars until every one she collected was full. "Then the oil stopped flowing" (2 Kings 4:6). The woman was able to sell the oil and pay off her debts.

Notice that the oil stopped flowing as soon as the last jar was full. God's provision was equal to the number of jars she collected, equal to the number of jars she believed God would fill.

In our limited understanding of God, we often place artificial limits on what we think He can accomplish. Our prayers become limited to what believe is actually possible. We may rejoice when our prayers are answered, but our level of faith has limited what God will provide.

We do serve an awesome God! He is more awesome than we can begin to comprehend. We must never think that there is a problem too big for Him to handle. "[He] is able to do immeasurably more than all we ask or imagine" (Ephesians 3:20).

We may doubt our own abilities, we may even set our own goals a bit too low, but let's trust Him to "meet all your needs according to his glorious riches in Christ Jesus" (Philippians 4:19). Believe, live, act, and pray as if He is truly the Creator of the universe, and let us refuse to place limits on God's provision. With Christ there are *no limits!*

PERFORMANCE PRINCIPLE 49

DECISIONS, DECISIONS

Recently a former Olympic champion and a highly regarded coach made the statement, "Your future as an athlete is much more dependent on what decisions you make, rather than on your genetic makeup."

Many athletes listen to the lies, "You're not big enough; You are too slow; You'll never make it in that league; You can't make the Olympic team!" Then they begin to believe the lies; "I can't do that; I'm not good enough to do that; I don't have the genetic makeup to bench 300 pounds; I haven't been gifted in that area."

Too many athletes make the self-defeating decisions of believing a lie, and then they live out the lie in their lives. They are defeated before they can prove the lie wrong.

Decisions cross our path like mosquitoes in a Minnesota summer. They fly all around us. There is no way to avoid them. In truth, failing to make a decision is making a decision. Even small decisions affect our everyday lives.

"Do I get up early and get a run in, or do I sleep in?

Do I bust my butt real hard in the weight room today, or do I slack off and just go through the motions?

Do I go to that party tonight, or do I study for that chemistry test?

Do I stay after practice and get some extra work in, or do I escape as soon as possible?

Even the small decisions you make mold and form your character. Those decisions over time then define your character.

The apostle Paul wrote that to win a race or even a boxing match, you need to make the decision to train your body and make it your slave. You have to learn mental toughness while you push beyond the threshold and barriers of pain. Paul said if you decide to compete, then you compete in such a way to win (1 Corinthians 9:24-26). That is a conscious decision that each athlete has to make. Only through tough, intensive, strict training can an athlete come near to victory. There are no shortcuts to the top.

Winning a race requires purpose and discipline. Paul uses this illustration to explain that the Christian life takes hard work, self-denial, and grueling preparation. As Christians, we are running toward our heavenly reward.

What are you running toward? Are you chasing after Jesus or the things of this world?

Now is the time to make a decision to live for Him. Don't put off the decision. Act now and keep your commitment. There is only one way to win in this life, and that is to know Him as personal Lord and Savior. It has nothing to do with your genetics, your strength, your speed, or how much you can bench press. This is a matter of heart and desire—to know and follow Him. This is the most important decision of your life. Simply ask Jesus to come into your life today, and He will—you won't be disappointed with the final results. He will give you the grace to win the real race and reach your full potential.

PERFORMANCE PRINCIPLE 50

WHY AM I HERE?

Have you ever been in a slump? Has the occasional loss become a streak? Has the labor of love become a tedious job? Do you have a hard time getting along with your coach or your athletic administrator? Are you getting the playing time, the scholarship, the salary, or the budget you think you deserve? Do you think you are getting the short end of the stick more than often enough? Have you muttered, *Why me?*

We all go through tough times. Oh yes, there are days when the grass looks so much greener on the other side of the fence. *How we desire to be there instead of here!* Those are the days when we demand a trade, update our resume, or desire to play the free agency market.

Have you wondered more than once, *Why am I here?*

For many of us, athletics is our total focus. We have a plan for almost everything we do. We are driven to reach the next level, and we are working the plan. Sometimes our focus is so narrow we define who we are by what we do, rather than who we are. We are immersed in sport, but it should not be our singular focus.

God's Word says, "The very steps we take come from God" (Proverbs 20:24, THE MESSAGE), and wherever God places us is not only part of His plan for our lives, but for the lives of those with whom we interact as well. It is possible that God will place us in schools, universities, professional teams and organizations, and companies that need our prayers and our witness.

Have you seriously considered that it may not be all about us, but about serving Him?

God always has a plan. What do you think would be the effect if we would be active participants in God's game plan, rather than purely following our own ambition or complaining from the sidelines? Why not seek to be a part of it?

We need to do our work as to the Lord as Paul says in Ephesians. "Don't just do what you have to do to get by, but work heartily, as Christ's servants doing what God wants you to do. And work with a smile on your face, always keeping in mind that no matter who happens to be giving the orders, you're really serving God" (Ephesians 6:6-7, THE MESSAGE).

There are eyes that continually observe the lives of those of us who claim the name of Christ. Sometimes they throw it in your face, but they always notice how you react in life. Maybe God placed you where you are right now because He is using your life to be a great witness to someone who is studying your pattern of behavior. Perhaps godly leadership is needed where you are. Maybe the joy that permeates your life is of vital importance to the plan God has to sweeten the environment around you. You will never know why you are where you are until you ask!

PERFORMANCE PRINCIPLE 51

Take a Stand

In the 1924 Olympic Games in Paris, Eric Liddell made the headlines when he refused to compete in his strongest event, the 100-meter dash, because the qualifying heats were held on Sunday.

Liddell was a deeply committed Christian. Like many in his day, he believed that Sunday should be set aside for worship, not worldly pursuits. Many people who agreed with Eric's conviction supported him. The British Olympic Committee even tried unsuccessfully to get the International Olympic Committee to change the date of the 100-meter heats. Yet, Liddell was not universally praised. His stand brought him criticism as well.

Yet, Liddell was prepared to sacrifice his dream of a 100-meter Gold medal for the sake of his moral principles and spiritual convictions.

Like Eric, we live in a world that can be hostile toward our beliefs and convictions. Behavior once considered shameful is now thought as normal. We are constantly confronted with profanity, sexually suggestive material, and opportunities to cheat or steal. It is not easy to take a stand for the things that we believe in.

When Olympic officials could not convince Liddell to run in the 100-meters on Sunday, he agreed to compete in the 200 and 400 meter races. In true storybook fashion, Eric won two Olympic medals: the bronze in the 200 meters, and the Gold in the 400 meters, setting an Olympic record in the process.

Jesus said, "Whoever acknowledges me before men, I will also acknowledge him before my Father in heaven" (Matthew 10:32). Clearly God honors those who honor Him.

No matter what people say, no matter if you win or lose, you cannot go wrong when you take a stand for your convictions.

PERFORMANCE PRINCIPLE 52

LISTEN TO COACH

I am sure that you have heard of "Wrong Way" Riegals. Roy Riegals played in the 1929 Rose Bowl for the University of California and made one of the most famous mistakes in the history of football.

Riegals picked up a fumble, and he looked up and saw a vast sea of green before him. He headed down the field toward the end zone more than 60 yards away—in the wrong direction! Finally he was tackled by his own teammates inside their own 10-yard line where they were forced to punt. Georgia Tech blocked the kick and scored.

At half-time, the California head football coach gave a rousing call to his disappointed and discouraged team. At the end of the half-time speech he declared, "Same team that started the first half will start the second half." That meant Roy Riegals was going to be put back in the game.

All the players ran out on the field except Roy. "Coach, I cannot go out there," Roy said. "I'm humiliated."

The coach looked in the face and said, "Roy, the game is only half over. Now get out there and play the rest of it."

The words of that coach are worth remembering today. We all have blown it. We all have made boneheaded mistakes in life and sport. Too often we feel like Roy did, like we cannot go back out there after our failure. But the truth of the matter is that there is a whole lot left to play. The choice is yours. You can pick yourself up and wipe away the disappointment and refocus your energy, or sit yourself down on the bench and feel sorry for yourself.

God, our Master Coach has a game plan for your life. He pulls us aside and says, "I know the plans I have for you, plans to prosper you and not harm you. Plans to give you hope and a future" (Jeremiah 29:11).

It is important to listen to our coach no matter what the circumstances or situation. We can't depend on our feelings, but we need to depend on His leadership. For it is His direction, guidance, and counsel that puts us in the best possible position for the ultimate victory. Listen to Coach.

PERFORMANCE PRINCIPLE 53

SO WHAT ARE YOU LOOKING AT?

In 1952, a very brave and strong young woman waded into the Pacific Ocean; Florence Chadwick was determined to break another record. Up to that time, no woman had ever crossed the channel between Catalina Island and the California coast. Long distance swimming wasn't new to Florence. She had, in fact, been the first woman to swim the English Channel in both directions.

This challenge was to be a 21-mile effort. The conditions were not perfect. Not only was the water incredibly cold, but a thick blanket of fog had settled in. To make matters worse, there were sharks that trailed her that had to be driven off several times!

Florence's coach and family followed in a small boat, cheering her on. "Go for it, Florence! You can do it," they shouted.

The problem that day turned out to be the fog. It was really foggy. Even after 15 hours of swimming, Florence still could not see the shoreline. Discouragement and fatigue began to set in. Florence finally took her last stroke, telling her coach that she just couldn't go on. She quit.

Her family and coach consoled her as they pulled her aboard the boat, and she collapsed with exhaustion.

As it turned out, Florence quit too soon that cold July morning. She swam 20.5 miles, but because she could not see the end—couldn't focus on the goal—Florence Chadwick fell short by a half mile. Had she been able to focus, the results would undoubtedly have been different. Focus is the state of clear definition, or the ability to concentrate on a specific area or idea. Focus allows you to function in a complicated environment. Without focus you would be overloaded with too much input from your senses. Finding the appropriate center of interest can be a challenge. The real problem begins when you focus on things that are not important, or when you fail to focus on the important areas. Focus can be a problem for any athlete, or for anybody; consider the disciple Peter for example.

One night on the Sea of Galilee (Matthew 14), while the disciples battled the wind and the waves alone in a small boat, they saw the form of a man walking on the water toward them. They were terrified.

But Jesus was quick to comfort them. "Courage, it's me. Don't be afraid," he called out to them. Peter, suddenly bold, said, "Master, if it is really you, call me to come to you on the water."

Jumping out of the boat, Peter walked on the water toward Jesus. But when he looked down and saw the wind and the waves, he lost focus and started to sink. He cried out to Jesus, "Master, save me!"

Peter was in the middle of an awesome display of God's power and yet he "saw the wind." Peter began to look at the world and not at the One who created the world, and he began to sink into the waves: "Let us fix our eyes on Jesus, the author and perfecter of our faith" (Hebrews 12:2).

There are times when we can clearly see God's hand at work. When our eyes become focused on Jesus, His peace fills our life, and the foundation under our feet feels solid and secure. However, it is usually not long before the wind begins to blow, the waves rise up, and we feel that sinking feeling. When this happens (and it will!) we must not despair; this is also part of God's wonderful plan. As we are sinking, He always offers an invitation to know Him better—to know He will always be there when we cry out, "Master, save me!"

The walk of faith cannot be accomplished by our own strength. With each step we must "put to death whatever belongs to your earthly nature" (Colossians 3:5), and "clothe yourselves with the Lord Jesus Christ" (Romans 13:14).

Every day we must refocus, taking our eyes off our own abilities and the desires of the world, to a committed, trusting, singular focus on Jesus. The question remains, "So what are you looking at?"

PERFORMANCE PRINCIPLE 54

WHO'S IN CONTROL?

Building a winning program is a tough challenge. So many factors play a part in success in sport. A number of years ago, when I got my first collegiate head coaching job, I was determined to build a winning program. I felt I knew the way to success after serving as assistant coach for 11 years, and having been around successful athletic programs in high school and college as an athlete.

I worked extremely hard to recruit and bring in the best talent available. I recruited nonstop, making late-night phone calls, driving all over the Midwest, and flying from Arizona to Florida to convince these 18-year-old kids to believe in my dream of creating a championship team. I got athletes. Maybe they were not the most talented, but they had a solid work ethic, they were mentally tough, and they know how to win. I got an assistant coach who was talented and tough too. The pieces began to fall together. I couldn't wait for the season to begin. On paper we were young and inexperienced, but the potential was there for greatness.

I saw what we had and what we could be. I knew what we had—a team that would win championships for years, a team that would produce All-Americans and maybe a few national champions. We went to our first tournament of the season and we had 10 wrestlers win medals—all freshman and sophomores! The next week we dueled the number-three-ranked team in the nation, and we pounded them 49-0! Oh, man, we had created something special.

Then the unthinkable happened. A prank between teammates turned into a national nightmare. Seven athletes were arrested and charged with felonies, including my assistant coach.

Another athlete was charged with arson when he torched my garage and van, angry that the assistant coach was fired and that his teammates were expelled from school.

I went, in a heartbeat, from the proud creator of a successful athletic program—a program that was second to none—to a guy who wanted to hide in the nearest cave. When Oprah called, I did not want to talk to her! Everyone avoided me, even my fellow collegiate coaches kept their distance. It was as though I had the plague. I found out that I had little or no control of anything that was happening around me. I felt helpless.

No amount of our own sweat and blood can ever create *the ideal.* When we strive to build and create, we are chasing after the world's elusive, ever changing false definition of what is really fulfilling and ideal. I have climbed the mountains of worldly athletic pursuit, stood on the very summit, and found that there is nothing fulfilling and ideal there. Nothing. As I turned a full 360 degrees, I realized that the path in every direction leads into a deep valley.

The absolute best in life begins when we realize our life belongs to Christ, and that life must be surrendered to Him to create the life He desires for us. "I have been crucified with Christ and I no longer live" (Galatians 2:20).

We were created by Jesus for His sovereign purpose, "We are the clay, you are the potter; we are all the work of your hand" (Isaiah 64:8). Unfortunately, somewhere along the way, we began to consider ourselves as the work of our own hands. We even tried to create according to the world's system. We tried to fulfill our own *needs,* and fight for our own *rights,* time and time again. The losses pile up, *not* the victories.

The truth that will set us free is the understanding that our needs are extremely small and that we actually have *no* rights. "You are not your own; you were bought at a price" (1 Corinthians 6:19-20). We have been purchased with the blood of Jesus. His gift to us as joint heirs to His Kingdom is eternal life. We need and deserve nothing more.

If we truly want the ideal, the best, we will stop trying to create our life, our program, our career and place every area of our lives into the hands of a loving Creator instead. The ideal job is ours for the asking. The ideal program, the ideal coaching staff, the ideal family, the ideal marriage and friends are all ours—but only through the releasing of our rights and by redefining our needs. We only need to humbly understand WHO is in control.

PERFORMANCE PRINCIPLE 55

GOING IT ALONE

Jackie Berube of Escanaba, Michigan is a gifted athlete. In high school she was a talented gymnast who went on to compete in the sport at the University of Wisconsin-La Crosse. At UW-L, Berube was introduced to the world of women's wrestling and found a niche there, and she pursued the sport with intensity and passion. Soon Jackie was a US national champion and won a Silver medal in the 1996 World Championships.

When Jackie was training as a wrestler, she took a job as an intern in the weight room of the US Olympic Training Center in Colorado Springs. It was there that Jackie fell in love with the weights. In 1998, Jackie was offered a spot in the Olympic Training Center Resident program for women's weight lifting. Jackie jumped after the opportunity, even though she had to quit her full-time job as a strength coach and give up wrestling.

For two years she diligently trained, hoping to make the 2000 Olympic Games in Sydney. She fell short of her goals. She picked up the disappointment, refocused on her goals, and trained with renewed passion. In 2001 she qualified for the World Championships in Anatayla, Turkey. But when terrorist attacks on New York and Washington hit on September 11th, USA Weightlifting announced that it was not safe to travel to Turkey and that it was not going to send a team to the championships.

Jackie Berube said she was going! She would do whatever it took to get to the World Championships. She would be going it alone. Berube, the only American in the World Weightlifting Championships, finished fifth after overcoming a heavy burden of another kind. "I had to pay for my trip out of my own pocket," she said. "I thought it was very important that I come and represent my country."

Going it alone can be a tough burden. It can be tough if you are the only Christian on your team, the only Christian in the office, the only Christian on the coaching staff. Going it alone is tough. But like Jackie Berube, we need to overcome the challenge. We need to fight for what we believe in. We need to say no to the world and say yes to what Christ wants us to do. That means fixing our eyes on Jesus and persevering in our situations.

Sometimes the burden is a heavy one to carry. The cost of following Christ is expensive. The teasing, the nasty words, the jokes produce a painful scar. Yet in our suffering a real lasting character is produced. James tells us that we are to "Consider it pure joy, my brothers whenever you face trials of many kinds, because you know that the testing of your faith develops perseverance. Perseverance must finish its work so that you may be mature and complete, not lacking anything" (James 1:2-4).

Anyone who meets a challenge head-on and manages to stick it out is a champion. In God's eyes, for such a person who is loyally in love with Him and committed to Him, the reward is life and more life. The prize is so much worth the effort and the sacrifice.

PERFORMANCE PRINCIPLE 56

NOTHING TOO HARD

Before I graduated from college, I wanted to do my student teaching under a top-notch Christian coach. One day I read an article on Jim Rexilius of Wheaton, Illinois, in the Fellowship of Christian Athlete magazine, *The Christian Athlete.* I knew of Coach Rex while I was in high school. He was a tough, disciplined, demanding ex-Marine who knew how to win. I wrote to Coach Rex and asked to do my student teaching under him. I also asked for the opportunity to be involved with the Wheaton North football program, which had dominated the always tough DuPage Valley Conference.

I had a wonderful opportunity that year. I learned so much from my mentor. We had a great team that had two future number one NFL draft choices. We marched through the regular season with an undefeated record, making it to the state semifinals. The year also had its rough moments. I remember watching Coach Rex suspend 15 seniors for one game for breaking team rules. To him, it did not matter if we were undefeated or not. You had to do the right thing. There was no compromise. There was no doubt that Coach Rex was a man of character and integrity.

Coach Rex moved on after the season to take the head coaching position at Wheaton College. He helped me get his former high school teaching job after I graduated in December. Then the following August, I joined him at the college as the offensive line coach. It was a move and opportunity for which I will forever be grateful.

I learned a lot from my two seasons with Coach Rex. He took a lump of clay and molded me into a coach, but more importantly, a Christian coach who learned not only how to coach and motivate, but to love his athletes as well. Everywhere I have been over the last 23 years, into each new position, I have taken the lessons Coach Rex taught me.

Coach Rex never retired. He would volunteer coach at a local high school, and he continued leading a Fellowship of Christian Athlete huddle group in the basement of his home and help kids get to FCA camp each summer. When most are retired and kicking back, Coach Rex was in the battle each day.

One day I got an E-mail from Coach Rex. He was diagnosed with a fast-spreading form of liver cancer. He requested that I pray for him.

Man, you just want to get angry and ask God why? Why would He let this happen to such a good guy, to a man who loves God so much? Why would He allow this to happen to a man who has given so much to so many during his coaching career?

In the 32nd chapter of Jeremiah, God told Jeremiah to purchase a field from his cousin. This was a very strange and unusual command. For almost 40 years, Jeremiah had been warning the people of Jerusalem to repent of their sin or face destruction by the Babylonians. Now the end was near: "the king of Babylon was then besieging Jerusalem" (Jeremiah 32:2). The enemy had occupied the land all around the city, yet God told Jeremiah to buy a field.

Jeremiah obediently purchased the property, but then he questioned God's reasoning. "See how the siege ramps are built up to take the city...though the city will be handed over to the Babylonians, you...say to me, 'Buy the field" (Jeremiah 32:24-25). Even though Jeremiah had been a prophet and had talked to God for years, this action did not make sense to him.

God answered Jeremiah with a simple, yet challenging question. "Is anything too hard for me?" (Jeremiah 32:27).

Yes, the enemy had invaded the land and would soon overrun the city, but God's plan was for the people to return one day, "and let them live in safety. They will be my people, and I will be their God" (Jeremiah 32:37-38). Jeremiah's field was a reminder that God would one day restore His people, a reminder that He could be trusted even in the face of overwhelming circumstances.

We often have a difficult time seeing how all the pieces of God's plan fit together. The enemy attacks and we don't understand why. We want to fight back, but God says to trust Him and pray. We want to solve the problems, but God says to love Him and share His love with others.

Let's put over lives in His hands and submit to His guidance, even when we may not see where we're going or how we are going to get there. And let's always remember—for God, there is *nothing* too hard.

PERFORMANCE PRINCIPLE 57

LET YOUR YES BE YES

Not too long ago I got a call from USA Wrestling. One of their coaches who was assigned to a two-week wrestling tour to China couldn't make the trip due to personal business reasons. I was asked if I could replace him on the trip. I was thrilled, and very excited about the prospect to coach overseas and to travel to China. Immediately I said, "YES!," without looking at my calendar or previous commitments.

Later I noticed I had a commitment to do a five-day commuter wrestling camp at a high school in the Twin Cities area. It had been a fun camp in the past and I like doing it. The thing was the pay—around $500 for 15 hours of work. I could use the money, but a trip to China…well that was the trip of a lifetime.

I got on the phone right away to see if I could reschedule the camp. Unfortunately, that was not an option. I explained the situation to the camp coordinator. They then asked if I could line up another college coach to take my place. I made some calls and finally got a former athlete of mine who was coaching in college, to replace me at the camp.

Now I had to get a visa application for entry into China, get a passport-sized photo for the application, and express-mail everything to the Chinese consulate in New York. I filled out the application, had the photo taken, and went to the post office with my materials, and I included a return express-mail envelope. I did everything the way I was instructed. Now I had to wait and the time was running out.

With a Monday flight out of Minneapolis to Los Angles, I was tense while I awaited the mail delivery on Saturday. When the mail finally arrived, there was no package from the Chinese consulate! I rushed down to my local post office and explained my situation to the postmaster. He told me I could go to the central distribution center (60 miles away) and see on Sunday if the express-mail package had arrived for Monday delivery. Other than that there was not much they could do.

On Sunday afternoon I made the hour drive to the distribution center. I parked my car and found a couple of postal service workers around back who were sitting on the loading dock taking a break. I told them my story. One of the workers got up and went inside to see what he could find. He was gone about five minutes, and when he returned he had an express-mail package in his hand!

I jumped into the car and headed home ready to pack my bags for China. As I was driving I glanced over at the package a couple of times. I then decided to open it up and look through the materials in the envelope. I pulled out the cover letter and began to read it—I had been denied a visa! I was stunned. The letter stated in detail that I did not follow the proper procedure, thus I was denied entry to China.

I called USA Wrestling and explained what had just happened. We looked at the options of getting a visa in Tokyo, but that seemed so daunting to me. Given that, there was no way around it. I wouldn't be making the trip. Unfortunately, I was informed that I had all the visas for the team in my possession, and that I had to deliver them to the team or else they would not gain entry to China either. So I had to drive three hours to Minneapolis on Monday morning, park and deliver the visas to the team leader at the airport gate, then drive three hours back home.

Understandably, I was very disappointed. No coaching trip to China. I was out $500 for canceling the wrestling camp position, out for a six-hour round-trip to Minneapolis, plus airport parking. I was out the money for a passport photo, and out the cost of the visa application and two express-mail envelopes! Out a day of productive work! I was upset!

On the way home from Minneapolis, I told God how disappointed I was. His reply was simply, "Let your 'Yes' be 'Yes,' and your 'No' be 'No'" (Matthew 5:37). He didn't need to say another word. I knew exactly what He was talking about.

God has a playbook that He expects us to follow. It is called the Bible. As members on His team, we are expected to know and follow the playbook. In fact, we are accountable for everything in the book.

As a college and high school football coach, I have on numerous occasions yanked guys from the game for mental mistakes—for not knowing their assignments. Now I realized that I got yanked by God from a trip to China for messing up an assignment. It was a hard way to learn a lesson, but let me tell you, I did learn from it.

God expects us to be men and women of integrity. Our words and our commitments are important. If we say we are going to do something, we better do it! In the Old Testament it is written, "When a man makes a vow to the LORD or takes an oath to obligate himself in a pledge, he must not break his word but must do everything he said" (Numbers 30:2).

Promises must be kept, deadlines must be met, commitments honored, not for the sake of morality, but because we become what we do, or fail to do. Our character is the sum of all that.

"Let your yes be yes" is an assignment we cannot afford to mess up. Our goal is to be a person of word and action. We cannot simply say we will do something, but we need to *do* it—doing it with a love and passion in such a way as to honor our Lord, Jesus Christ.

PERFORMANCE PRINCIPLE 58

WHAT IS YOUR LIFE?

Green Bay's Brett Favre might be described as a hard-headed throwback to another era of professional football. Favre is the kind of guy who after a quarterback sack, bounces up, congratulates his pursuer with a rap on the top of his helmet, then goes back to business of frustrating the opposing defense. Favre is a warrior who wages battle often beyond his physical limitations, embodying everything that is attractive and addictive about this brutal sport called football.

Some say he's tough. Others say he's talented. Most say he's crazy. Brett Favre, a three-time NFL Most Valuable Player and Super Bowl Champion, is without question, one of the most exciting and electric players in the National Football League today, adding both personality and spark to the sport.

In the 2002 season, Favre was moved to tears when he was driven off the field in a golf cart by the medical staff with a strained knee ligament. His knee had been awkwardly twisted in the Lambeau Field turf as Washington Redskin linebacker LaVar Arlington sacked him for a loss. Favre left the field crying, not because he was in pain or because he couldn't play. It wasn't about keeping his starting game streak alive either; it was about quenching that never-satisfied thirst for the fight.

"We all can be lulled to sleep sometimes by being able to play every week and overcoming injuries," said Favre. "But I am very aware that at any point it could be taken away. Some people may say that this was a wake-up call, but I've said all along, hey, you're just a hit away."

Like Brett Favre, we are all just a hit away. In a moment, in the blink of an eye, life can change for all of us.

James writes, "What is your life? You are a mist that appears for a little while and then vanishes" (James 4:14).

The question, "What is your life?" demands a response. Where are you placing all your trust? In the game? In your job? On your good looks? On your academics? On your portfolio? Just exactly where is your trust?

Jesus said, "Therefore everyone who hears these words of mine and puts them into practice is like a wise man who builds his house on the rock. The rain came down, the streams rose, and the winds blew and beat against that house; yet it did not fall, because it had its foundation on the rock. But everyone who hears these words of mine and does not put them into practice is like a foolish man who built his house on sand. The rain came down, the streams rose, and the winds blew and beat against that house, and it fell with a great crash" (Matthew 7:24-27).

What are you building your life upon? The rock or the sand? Take some time to do some critical evaluation before you answer this question.

We need to be like the wise man and trust in the words of Christ, and then put them to work in our lives. When we do that, we build the foundation of our life on the rock. A secure foundation will withstand the loss of jobs, severe knee injuries, the loss of investments, and even death itself. Nothing, no nothing, can beat down what we build upon the rock of Christ.

"What is your life?" is a good question. What's your answer?

PERFORMANCE PRINCIPLE 59

SHARPEN YOUR GAME

Kerry Wood of the Chicago Cubs was the 1998 Rookie of the Year in the National League. Wood put up some great numbers: 223 strikeouts, a record-tying 20 strikeout game versus the Houston Astros, and an opponent batting average (against him) of .196. Wood also earned a 13-6 record with a 3.4 earned run average—not common rookie statistics in the least! But in his sophomore season, Wood suffered a torn ligament in his right elbow during spring training and was lost for the season.

Kerry Wood made it back to the big leagues in the spring of 2000. It took a lot of painful, hard work to recover completely from the injury and to survive rehab, but Kerry Wood persevered.

Wood struggled early in the 2000 season. His earned run average soared to over 7.0 during May and June. Many critics argued that he would never regain his rookie form, the control he had, his blazing fastball, or his wicked curveball.

As the season wore on, Kerry slowly regained his form and his confidence. By September, Wood's ERA had dropped to 4.8. He finished the season with a 8-7 record with 23 starts and 132 strikeouts.

In Ecclesiastes 10:10 it is written: "Since a dull axe requires great strength, sharpen the blade. That's the value of wisdom; it helps you succeed."

In athletics, trying to do anything without the necessary skills or tools is like chopping wood with a dull axe. Much effort will be required. If your athletic skills or techniques are dull, you need to sharpen them to do a more efficient job. How do you accomplish this? By sharpening them through the grinding of training and repetition.

It took Kerry Wood months to sharpen his skills to return to form. Likewise you need to recognize where a problem exists, then go to work on honing those skills. You not only need to evaluate the athletic areas, but all the areas of your life where your "axe" may be dull. Your effectiveness is on the line—stay sharp!

PERFORMANCE PRINCIPLE 60

PROPER PROGRESSION

Coach Carl "Buck" Nystrom was once called by *Sports Illustrated* magazine, "the best offensive line coach in the country." This man coached and developed champions in some of the best college football programs in America: the University of Oklahoma, North Dakota State University, Northern Michigan University, the University of Colorado, and Michigan State University. The secret of Coach Buck's success was that every day, in every practice, he drilled the proper progression of line blocking into his athletes' minds so that it would become an automatic part of these linemans game skills.

The drill always started with the proper stance, then progressed to a trademark explosive start off the line on the quarterback's snap count. Then it progressed to "the fit" of the block (the proper blocking position relative to your opponent), and then, finally, to the essential leg drive completely through that opponent. These basic skills—the proper progression of run blocking skills turned "dogs into champions," as he used to say in his gruff tone of voice.

Every day, from the heat of August to the bone-chilling days of late November, Coach Buck drilled the proper progression of these skills. It was his secret of success, which consistently transformed his players into championship teams. In the Old Testament book of Haggai, God also shows us His proper progression.

The book of Haggai tells the story of the return of Israel

from exile in Babylon, and the rebuilding of Jerusalem and the temple. A problem that needed to be addressed was that the Jews were more concerned about getting their own homes rebuilt than God's temple. They had the order pretty seriously mixed up.

God told them, "Give careful thought to your ways. Go up into the mountains and bring timber and build the house (God is referring here to the house of God, the temple), so that I may take pleasure in it and be honored" (Haggai 1:7-8).

Israel did not prosper because their progression was wrong. God, in turn, blew away all of the possible results. "Why?" declares the Lord. "Because of my house, which remains a ruin, while each of you is busy with his own house." (Haggai 1:9). God's progression is to put Him first—above all other plans, interests, or pleasures.

Today God doesn't reside in a temple, but He lives in the hearts of those who love Him. If you want to do things right, there is only one way to do so—with proper progression. It all starts with giving honor and glory to God. The secret of success is putting God first!

PERFORMANCE PRINCIPLE 61

ARE YOU BRAVE ENOUGH?

Pat Tillman was a walk-on football player at Arizona State University. He proved himself that year (1994) earning both a starting position in the defensive secondary and a full-ride football scholarship. Before he was through with college Tillman proved something else to the entire Pac 10 Conference by being honored as the Most Valuable Defensive Player in the league.

The hard-hitting, 5-foot-11-inch, 202-pound safety with a big heart was then selected by the Arizona Cardinals in the 1998 NFL draft. It didn't take Tillman long to become the starting safety for the Cardinals. In the 2000 NFL season the 25-year-old veteran posted an incredible 224 tackles—setting a new team record.

Tillman always walked to a different beat. Although his promising football career was just beginning, he wasn't caught up in pursuing personal fame and the negotiations of a bigger contract as were many of his peers. In fact, Pat Tillman turned his back on the glitter and glory of professional football to pursue another calling.

Tillman declined a three-year $3.6 million contract in favor of joining the US Army! His decision is striking when you consider the financial realities. Tillman was just married a few months before that, but instead of making more than a million dollars a season with the Cardinals, Tillman would start at $18,000 a year with the Army.

ESPN concluded that Tillman's move was not a publicity

stunt, as he has refused all requests for media interviews—he just wanted to be a plain everyday soldier.

According to family and friends, Tillman's decision to join the Army sprung from a deep sense of duty and a simple desire to follow his conscience. ESPN reported that, "Tillman's conscience would not allow him to tackle opposing fullbacks when there was still a bigger enemy that needed to be stopped in its tracks."

One of Tillman's teammates offered a pithy but inspiring explanation for his reasoning. "He is," said Cardinal free safety Kwamie Lassiter, "a man who loves his country."

The question that remains for you is, *Are you brave enough to follow your convictions, no matter what the cost?*

Jesus challenged the conviction of His disciples when He said, "If anyone would come after me, he must deny himself and take up the cross and follow me. For whoever wants to save his life will lose it, but whoever loses his life for me will find it. What good will it be for a man if he gains the whole world, yet forfeits his soul?" (Matthew 16:24-26).

Commitment comes without compromise—it means pledging our whole being into service for the King. If we try to protect ourselves from the pain of suffering or loss, we may begin to die spiritually. Our lives may just turn inward as a result, losing our focus and intended purpose. When we give our life in service to Christ, however, we discover the real purpose of living.

Our convictions must be so strong that we are willing to turn our backs on the pleasures of the world and our own ambitions to follow Christ—even to the cross. Following Christ, therefore, means a true commitment, even the risk of death if necessary—and no turning back. I hope that some day someone will say of you, "He is certainly a person who loves His God."

PERFORMANCE PRINCIPLE 62

WHAT WE REALLY LONG FOR

Athletes from all sports are looking to improve and to maximize their performance. Setting goals plays a vital part in the mental edge and maximum performance of an athlete. Take away an athlete's goals and you will probably notice a big decline in motivation.

Goal setting is a very powerful tool that can yield valuable returns in all areas of your life, including your athletic performance. At its simplest level, the process of setting goals allows you to choose where you want to go in life and in your athletic career. By knowing what you want to achieve, you now have a guide to show you what to concentrate on and improve upon. Goal setting gives you long-term vision as well as short-term motivation.

By setting sharp, clearly defined goals, you can measure and take pride in the achievement of those goals. You can see forward progress in what might previously have seemed a long pointless grind.

Each of us is striving toward success. It matters not how we define success; we all pursue it in our own special way and for our own special reasons. We may dig deep, striving to reach the next level in hopes of greater recognition, achieving a free college education, earning more money, or just attaining the personal satisfaction of reaching our true potential.

Unfortunately, we are being trained to set goals, pursue them, reach them, then set new goals, all without evaluating what we truly need. In the pursuit of goal attainment, we must realize that reaching any goal will never, ever, result in total satisfaction. The bottom line is that we are all seeking something much greater, and in today's world, there is something even more elusive—a sense of peace and contentment.

We will never obtain true peace by attaining championships, records or recognition. Nor will it be found in a better job, school, or program. It can't be purchased or bought. True peace begins with the forgiveness of sins through faith in Jesus and grows as we live in submission to the Holy Spirit, "The mind of sinful man is death, but the mind controlled by the Spirit is life and peace" (Romans 8:6).

The apostle Paul coached the Philippians in the basic strategy of obtaining a life of peace: "Rejoice in the Lord always. I will say it again: Rejoice! Let your gentleness be evident to all. The Lord is near. Do not be anxious about anything, but in everything, by prayer and petition, with thanksgiving, present your requests to God. And the peace of God, which transcends all understanding, will guard your hearts and your minds in Christ Jesus" (Philippians 4:4-7).

Paul's strategy for peace is a simple game plan for success:
Rejoice
Rejoice some more!
Be gentle
Know God is near
Remove all anxiety
Pray about everything with a thankful heart. Jesus promised that those who trust in Him will receive a Peace beyond anything the world can understand, "Peace I leave with you; my peace I give you. I do not give to you as the world gives. Do not let your hearts be troubled and do not be afraid" (John 14:27).

If your life is lacking peace, the only solution is to draw nearer to God, trust Him more, and rejoice as you are guided by His Spirit. Only then can we find the success we have been longing and striving for. Only then will you obtain what your heart truly longs for—the true peace of God!

PERFORMANCE PRINCIPLE 63

NOT YOU, BUT...

I read the sports page in many newspapers from cover to cover. Usually in the back couple of pages you can find the transaction section for college and professional sports. You will notice as each season winds down more and more coaches have been asked to resign or have been fired from their positions. The season didn't go as well as expected. The alumni are not happy. The ticket sales are down. Often, the team didn't beat the hated rival, and all of this can add up to job loss for coaches who ended up on the wrong end of the expectations. The pressure to win is intense—it is the nature of the beast.

I was once hired on to a new football coaching staff where the outgoing staff went 8-3 for three straight seasons and got fired! They were great people and darn good coaches. The bottom line was that they didn't win enough to keep the boosters and the administration happy!

Typically, all the thinking is very optimistic when this urge to replace an incumbent coach takes over. The excitement builds as the search committee anticipates pumping new blood into the program. The arrangements get underway, and as the new candidates begin to come forward; everyone is full of hope about a new era of future success. When the decision is made, and a new coach steps up to the helm, everyone is happy and thrilled with the promise of greater accomplishments. The new coach and his staff are given carte blanche while the old staff couldn't get the concessions it desperately needed. Deal with it. This is just part of life in sport today.

The old coach is out of a job and we rarely think much about what happens next to those who have been replaced. There is a scramble to try and find a new position. Whether or not it is a coaching job, or something in a completely different field remains to be seen. The family may have to sell their home and move to a less expensive locale or someplace where an opportunity promises renewed stability. Meanwhile the kids get uprooted from their schools and lose the friends they love. Spouses must deal with the loss of friends and neighbors, the support of loving fellowship at church, and maybe even the loss of a job. Their whole world is turned upside down based on the performance of 19 and 20 year-old kids. It is tempting to point fingers and blame others.

Losing your job is tough. Bum Phillips, the great coach of the old Houston Oilers once said, "There are two kinds of coaches. Them that have been fired, and them that have not been fired yet." Well said.

We all experience different degrees of adversity in our lives. Consider the Old Testament character of Joseph for a moment. The especially beloved son of Jacob was sold into slavery by his jealous and scheming brothers. Then as a servant in Potiphar's house, a wealthy official from the court of Pharaoh, he is falsely accused and sentenced to jail (Genesis 39:20).

When a great famine struck the land of Egypt and even as far away as where Joseph had grown up, Joseph's brothers were sent to Egypt by his father Jacob in search of food. Because Joseph had carefully stored much grain against the time of famine, there was plenty to eat in Egypt and his brothers were to appear before the prime minister to make their request for famine relief. They had no idea that it was their brother Joseph, whom they had so terribly wronged.

After playing with them for a time, Joseph finally revealed himself to the very brothers who had betrayed him. They were terrified, but Joseph said, "So then, *it was not you who sent me here, but God.* He made me father to Pharaoh, lord of his entire household and ruler of all Egypt" (Genesis 45:8).

It is amazing to see how God, in His wonderful wisdom, ordered the events of the world for the good of Joseph, his family, and ultimately, His own glory. The apostle Paul presents the same principle when he wrote, "And we know that in all things God works for the good of those who love him, who have been called according to his purpose" (Romans 8:28).

As with Joseph, God is doing the same work in the lives of people today. We need to realize that as believers in Christ, all things do work together for our very own good! If you do believe and understand this important principle, then you cannot be depressed about your own situation, whatever befalls you.

Whether success or failure, whether in victory or defeat, whether hired or fired, God is ruling over the events in your life *for your good,* for the good of your family, and for the good of your friends, teammates, coaches, and associates; and for His own ultimate glory.

What does God have in store for you today? Can you say like Joseph, "not you, but by God" has this happened. May the Lord help you today to see that His amazing love and wonderful wisdom are working all things together for your own good.

PERFORMANCE PRINCIPLE 64

JUST RIGHT

In the world of sports psychology, activation plays an important part in whether or not an athlete is ready for competition. Simply put, activation is the skill of making appropriate physical and mental preparation so that an athlete can perform at his highest level. But activation can be tricky too. An athlete can become over prepared to take the field—too fired up if you will—and thereby actually diminish his performance. Of course, being inadequately fired up is a problem too. Being either too hot or too cold can negatively affect a performance.

Sports psychologists like to use the terms "activated" and "aroused" when discussing how excited, or how ready an athlete is for competition. Performance theory suggests that an athlete has an optimum level of arousal. We always knew that if a competitor goes into a game too relaxed, or too cold, that the performance level drops. When an athlete gets too hot—too fired up—he becomes overloaded with stress and worry. Either way, too hot or too cold, the athlete can lose focus and performance can suffer.

The key is for athletes to discover the optimal level of arousal. When everything is mentally and physically just right, then athletes perform at their very best. At that point of "just rightness" we could say that they are in a kind of "zone." Reaching this perfectly balanced place of preparation is no easy task. It is hard to get everything perfect—just right, but when things are—look out! That's when athletes seem to almost fly. Or sometimes it seems as though they know where to move before the next play has hardly begun. That is when we excel, when our performance is better than we could have imagined.

We have a loving Father in heaven, who has given us a gift that is just right to prepare us to live the greatest life imaginable. James tells us that, "Every good and perfect gift is from above" (James 1:17). This gift God has given us is precisely what we need to live—it is JUST RIGHT! If we only knew, we could be in a kind of heavenly zone. If we only realized what the gift was, we would rip it open immediately and receive it with a jump and a shout of joy! There in our hands would be the most perfect gift imaginable. You have most likely seen the gift before, and you might have even picked it up and given it a shake or two. But in the end you may have put the gift on a shelf and never thought to open it and find out what was inside.

In our lives we approach God for many things. We may ask Him to heal our ailing bodies, we may ask for a job we desire, we may come before Him asking Him to bless our performance, or perhaps just a chance to be in the starting lineup. Too often though, we ask for things we think would make our own personal world better. In the fourth chapter of the book of John, Jesus told the Samaritan women at the well that, "If you knew the gift of God and who it is that asks you for a drink, you would have asked him and he would have given you living water" (John 4:9).

We don't know what we truly need. It is ironic that, many times, we don't even ask for the things we need the most. We live life at a sub-par level of performance, where things are just not right at any level. In fact, we are not even close to the zone.

God's "just-right" gift for each of us is that same living water He offered to the women at the well. This gift is our salvation, the perfect transformation of our heart, and eternal life with Him. It is the forgiveness of sins, but it also refers to His ongoing gift of a victorious life of peace and contentment. Jesus answered, referring to the well where the women were going to draw drinking water, "Everyone who drinks the water I give him will never thirst" (John 4:13-14).

God's gift is free, but you need to openly receive the gift to possess it.

God has great plans for each of us, and His plans are much bigger and brighter than anything we can accomplish through our own strength and efforts. Take a free gift of God off the shelf today, a gift personally ideal for you in every way. Receive His gift. It is just what you need. It is just right!

PERFORMANCE PRINCIPLE 65

CHEERS FROM THE SIDELINES

Have you ever been to a cross-country race? If you haven't, you really should attend one. My favorite cross-country races in collegiate athletics are the Lester Park Invitational in Duluth, and the Roy Girak Invitational in Minneapolis, Minnesota.

It is early fall. The weather is cooling and brisk. The trees are full of God's palette of colors. At the starting line, which stretches almost a hundred meters, the teams gather in their assigned starting boxes. The athletes stretch, bounce, and take some starts and sprints to prepare themselves mentally for the challenge ahead of them. They huddle up, then do a team cheer; and then line up awaiting the starter's gun to fire. In just an instant they are off, funneling down the path, weaving around, over and through the golf course.

Lining the course are coaches with stopwatches and clipboards, parents, grandparents, siblings, boyfriends and girlfriends, classmates, teammates, and overall fans of the sport. At every turn the fans line up sometimes three to four deep. Voices scream out encouragement from the sidelines, "Keep you head up!... Nice pace… Use your arms… Push yourself!... Increase your stride… Pick off the two in front of you."

As the pack makes its way around the course pressing towards the finish line, other runners trail behind. Some are hurting physically; others struggle mentally as they fight the pain and the fatigue—the course has taken a toll on them. What is amazing to me is that the fans rise up and cheer for these athletes who will not even score a point in the team race—athletes they don't even know! It doesn't matter what colors they are wearing or what team they are representing. Fans cheer them on to the finish line. "Keep going, you're doing great! Way to run! You can do it!"

The eleventh chapter of Hebrews is often referred to as the Great Hall of Faith. The chapter begins with a clear definition of faith: "Now faith is being sure of what we hope for and certain of what we do not see" (Hebrews 11:1). It then describes many people from the Old Testament who were commended for their faith: Abel, Noah, Abraham, Joseph, Moses, Gideon, Samson, and David.

At the end of the impressive list we read that even though they were faithful, "none of them received what they had been promised" (Hebrews 11:39). Their glory or reward is being postponed. "God had planned something far better for us, so that only together with us would they be made perfect" (Hebrews 11:40).

It is as though the faithful from the past are now watching with great excitement and anticipation, knowing that one day soon we will be "caught up together with them" (1 Thessalonians 4:17) to receive our eternal reward. This awesome picture of the faithful leads directly into chapter twelve of Hebrews.

"Therefore, since we are surrounded by such a great cloud of witnesses, let us throw off everything that hinders and the sin that so easily entangles, and let us run with perseverance the race marked out for us" (Hebrews 12:1).

This "cloud of witnesses which surround us" is made up of men and women of faith from Abel on through the prophets and apostles. As we run the race and sometimes stumble and fall, the witnesses of the past are cheering us on and encouraging our steps:

> Abel: "Give God your very best, His favor will shine on you" (Genesis 4:4).

Abraham: "God will lead the way, trust Him with everything" (Genesis 12:1).

Moses: "You're good enough to serve, God will provide the tools you need" (Exodus 3-4).

Ruth: "God will renew your life and sustain you" (Ruth 4:15).

David: "You can conquer that giant! God is at your side!" (1 Samuel 17:37).

Paul: "Keep running to the end. God is waiting for you at the finish line" (2 Timothy 4:5-7).

My Mom: "In God's strength and ability in you, you can do all things. Abraham grew strong in faith as he praised God, for he knew that what God promised He was able to do through Him. Praise Him this day for your coaching, for all your athletes, and all your wins and defeats."

The race is long and sometimes difficult, but we are definitely not alone. Let's run with perseverance, and when we become discouraged, let's listen for the cheers from the sidelines!

PERFORMANCE PRINCIPLE 66

HIT THE CUTOFF MAN

I love baseball. It is a game for the little guy and the big guy alike. I fell in love with the game at an early age. In fact, I have an old torn, black-and-white photograph of myself dressed in a miniature Boston Red Sox uniform while I am chewing on a baseball, barely a year old.

I still chew on baseball, but now more on the transactions, the home run and batting title races, the divisional races, and who's hot and who's not, rather on that horsehide cover. I could sit and watch the game all season long, and I miss seeing the game after the World Series is over. The game isn't boring to me. It is a game of skill, of strategy, of finesse, and of speed and power. I love sitting in the clubhouse and talking baseball, and batting practice is a thing of beauty. What a great game!

Over the years I have watched a lot of softball and Little League games as my kids have moved up through the ranks starting with T-ball. Each year you could see the coaches move the best athletes into the infield positions. The first baseman had to be able to catch a ball, the shortstop and third baseman had to be able field a grounder, and then make the long and accurate throw to first base. Other than having a good catcher behind the plate—so that the ball didn't go to the backstop after every pitch, these were the most important elements of a good defense.

The outfielders were the youngest on the team, usually first-year players. They just sort of hung out, swatted buzzing mosquitoes, watched geese fly overhead and picked an occasional dandelion or two. Rarely did a ball ever reach them at their post. As the kids grew up, outfielders became more and more important in the defensive scheme. When a ball was whacked to the fence, it became critical that the outfielders could field the ball and hit the cutoff man with a throw. A throw that was short or off-line meant a run or two was going to score. An accurate throw to the cutoff man would hold the runners and possibly prevent a run from scoring.

In our lives sin is a long ball that has backed us up to the fence. The problem we have is that we often misjudge the distance, the path of the ball, and sometimes we even overestimate our skills to make the play.

Like the kid in Little League who throws wildly into the infield without the use of a cutoff man, we often take on the burdens or deal with the temptations of life without the help of Christ.

Playing our own game, making decisions without following the standards of the game draws us away from God, and our relationship with Him can suffer. It is like being benched.

Our effectiveness is reduced because pride can affect our judgment—we might feel we need to throw directly to home plate to make a big play, but what we really need is to hit our cutoff man, Jesus. He is not only our mediator for salvation, but for our everyday struggles. "For there is one God, and one mediator between God and men, the man Christ Jesus, who gave himself as a ransom for all men—the testimony given in its proper time" (1 Timothy 2:5-6).

How many decisions have you made without prayer? How many times have you launched a long throw hoping to cut down the runner without hitting the cutoff man? Did you wing it without a prayer? Was your throw too short? Too high? Did it just dribble in too late?

Surely we can trust Jesus to guide our daily decisions? Too often, I am afraid we are like the little kid who throws wildly out of pride saying, "I can do it, I can make the big play!" What would happen to us, do you think, if we would allow Jesus to guide us even in the small decisions? Is it possible we could even win a Golden Glove because we are playing by God's standards?

In the dugout sits the Master Coach. Patiently, He is saying to you kid, "HIT THE CUTOFF MAN!"

WORDS OF OPPORTUNITY

In the 1972 college football season, Baylor trailed Texas Christian University 34-7. With a little more than eleven minutes left in the game, the Baylor offense began to stage an incredible comeback. The Bears scored three touchdowns, and with two minutes left in the game, Baylor trailed 34-28. With the ball in its possession, Baylor was driving again toward the goal line.

With a first down on the 15-yard line, quarterback Neil Jeffrey was guiding the offensive unit beautifully. On first down, Jeffrey tossed a pass for nine yards. The next play on second-and-one, from the six-yard line, lost four yards. On third-and-five, with 43 seconds left Baylor took its final timeout.

A pass play was called, and both primary receivers were covered. Jeffrey dumped the ball off to the tailback flaring out of the backfield. He cut back inside and lost three yards; the clock continued to run down. Now it was fourth and eight from the 11-yard line. Baylor needed either a touchdown or a first down.

Somehow Neal Jeffrey thought it was third down, and he was only thinking of stopping the clock. Jeffrey took the snap and threw the ball to stop the clock. The Baylor players looked dumbfounded and so did the TCU players. The terrible reality of the moment struck. Neil Jeffrey was in tears as he reached the sidelines, sobbing, "I thought it was third down."

In the locker room following the game, the only sound heard was the crying of a shaking Neil Jeffrey. Baylor head football coach Grant Teaff stood up and addressed the team. He said, “I want all of you to know that I believe Neil Jeffrey did a fabulous job for us.” Then the coach took a step toward Neil. “Neil, Neil! Get your head up! Look at me!”

Slowly Neil’s head rotated up, and as Neil’s eyes met Grant’s he said, “Neil, I want to say that I think you did a fantastic, unbelievable job. That is what I want to say.”

In the background one could hear the players saying, “We love you Neil!”

Coach Teaff had the opportunity to either destroy Neil Jeffrey or heal the wounds of crushing defeat. His gracious and affirming words set the stage for Baylor to win the Southwest Conference Football championship a year later. Everything we say has an effect on those around us. The effect is either positive or negative; very rarely are our words neutral.

Paul wrote to the Ephesians, “Do not let any unwholesome talk come out of your mouths, but only what is helpful for building others up according to their needs, that it may benefit those who are listen” (Ephesians 4:29).

This means that every time we speak, we have the opportunity to encourage and opportunity to minister. With just a few moments of our time and very little effort, we have the opportunity to brighten someone’s day, to lighten the load that they may be carrying, and possibly draw them closer to God. This precious opportunity must not be taken lightly.

Our words can be very effective as a source of encouragement, but they also can be used to cause great harm. “Like a madman shooting firebrands or deadly arrows is a man who deceives his neighbor and says, ‘I was only joking!” (Proverbs 26:18-19). Sarcastic and joking words are “deadly arrows,” which are never useful for “building others up.” Over time, this mode of communication can destroy a relationship or even a life.

Our words are a powerful gift. Let’s honor our heavenly Father by effectively using His gift to encourage. Let’s speak so that those who listen may benefit and be built up. Let’s not squander the opportunity of our words!

PERFORMANCE PRINCIPLE 68

STUDENT OF THE GAME

My good friend, Steve Fraser, is the head coach for the US Greco-Roman National team. Coach Fraser, a 1984 Olympic champion, has a sound philosophy concerning the importance of conditioning. Being in *great* shape is his philosophy.

Coach Fraser believes that when you have an opponent that is fast or quick, when he gets tired, he is no longer fast or quick. If your opponent is really strong, when he gets tired, he is no longer strong. If your opponent has great technique and gets tired, he no longer has great technique. If you can make an opponent tired, while you are not, you will be faster, stronger, and your technique will work better.

Coach Fraser teaches that you conquer fatigue by becoming the best athlete you can be. He always stresses that you need to continually work hard on your conditioning!

King Solomon also had a great philosophy concerning gaining the victory: "A wise man is mightier than a strong man. So don't go to war without wise guidance; victory depends on having many counselors" (Proverbs 24:5-6, NLT).

If an athlete has wisdom, if he can assess the situation, then plan strategy and tactics, he will develop an advantage over physically stronger but unwise opponents.

As an athlete, you train in a number of areas. You sharpen your technical skills. You develop your aerobic and anaerobic capacity. You pump iron to develop your strength and muscular endurance, and you make sound nutritional choices to fuel your body. Do you, however make a similar effort to develop wisdom and knowledge of your sport? You need to become a student of the game.

Because wisdom is a vital part of strength, it pays to attain it. If you are seeking victory, first seek wisdom!

PERFORMANCE PRINCIPLE 69

SINGLENESS OF PURPOSE

Whether it be the NBA Finals, the World Series, the Super Bowl, or the Stanley Cup, professional athletes of all sports desire "the ring." The championship ring signifies the achievement of having become a world champion. An entire career is wrapped up in the pursuit of "the ring."

Do you enjoy setting goals and achieving them? I do! I find goal setting and achievement to be intoxicating. A number of years ago I wrote up a list of coaching goals I wanted to pursue. One by one I knocked them out. When I finally reached a goal, I felt a deep sense of personal satisfaction. I loved the challenge. There was a thrill in climbing the mountain of my goals and planting the flag on top in victory. But like any mountain, you cannot stay on top, you have to come back down into the valley.

I found that the satisfaction in attainment only lasted moments—then suddenly the thrill, the high disappeared like a vapor. Then I craved more. That's one of the greatest problems in achievement goals; they become an unrelated string of hollow victories which are increasingly frustrating as more and more is achieved.

King Solomon had everything: wisdom, power, riches, honor, reputation, and God's favor. Solomon wrote this: "What do people get for all their hard work? Everything is so weary and tiresome!... No matter how much we hear, we are not content" (Ecclesiastes 1:3,8).

Solomon wrote this book after he tried everything and achieved much, only to find that nothing apart from God made him happy. Solomon wanted his readers to avoid these same senseless pursuits. If we are to find meaning in our accomplishments rather than in God, we will never be satisfied, and everything we pursue will become meaningless. Solomon concluded that the only true goal—the singleness of purpose is to know God (Ecclesiastes 12:13-14). We should search for purpose and meaning in life, but they cannot be found in human endeavors.

The true purpose is to know and serve God. In Colossians, Paul writes: "Work hard and cheerfully at whatever you do, as though you were working for the Lord rather than for people. Remember that the Lord will give you an inheritance as your reward, and the Master you are serving is Christ" (Colossians 3:23-24).

Our significance is found in giving our all for Christ in everything we do. Leave your selfish ambition at the foot of the cross, and now run ahead and give Christ all the glory in all that you do. He will bless you with a very rich and lasting inheritance.

PERFORMANCE PRINCIPLE 70

SEE HOW FAR YOU'VE COME

For the last 13 years, I have kept a training journal. A training journal is one of the secrets of success, which I learned long ago. It is an absolute must if you as a coach or as an athlete want to make the most of your training.

Boston marathon champion Bill Rodgers is quoted as saying, "To repeat successes of the past, follow your old program. Don't get fancy; just be consistent." That is so true. But to follow the old program that worked, you need to have written down what you did.

Keeping detailed accounts of practices, drills, exercises, and sets and reps of weights used in strength training help to remind me of what I or my team did on a certain day, week, or month—last year or 13 years ago. Those records allow me to review what worked, to evaluate what needed to be changed, and taught me lessons on how my team or I adapted to certain stressors that occurred during that season.

You may think that you will never forget a particular event or practice, but could you remember the exact workout or the days and weeks leading up to a big event? Every piece of the puzzle in training is important.

The greatest benefit of keeping a journal is the ability to look back over the past weeks, months, and years in order to recall and review the roadblocks and hurdles that were overcome, to think about how the adversity was defeated, and the strength and mental toughness that developed as a result of that particular routine. You can also see clearly just how far you have come.

There is another kind of journal that I recommend you keep also, a prayer journal. Over the years, I have jotted down notes of prayers, needs, and how God has responded in times of adversity. As I flip through some of these old journals, I can look back and see how God controlled events in order to mold and shape me through the fires of adversity. I can remember when a Bible verse hit me square in the face and melted into my heart, when I finally understood what it meant for the first time.

I can also reread stories about times when I could actually see God's hand at work and remember personal messages and lessons I've since forgotten. I have seen prayers instantly answered for broken bones and torn-up knees—seen them healed through simply faith. I have seen God touch a whole team, bringing them to sobbing tears as they met Jesus for the first time.

Oh, and there is that time when God answered my prayer to allow me to drive my car home from Duluth in spite of a blown-out transmission while on vacation. I rolled into my driveway five hours later and the car didn't move again on its own. And how about when I lost my coaching position at Michigan Tech University? I had no paycheck coming in, and I'd been out of work for six months. My wife was pregnant with our third child, and I was making payments on a new car; but somehow, some way, there was food on the table, our bills got paid, and we survived the storm. It was all God. That is the only way to describe it.

Listen to what God said generations ago, "Fix these words of mine in your hearts and minds; tie them as symbols on your hands and bind them on your foreheads. Teach them to your children, talking about them when you sit at home and when you walk along the road, when you lie down and when you get up. Write them on the doorframes of your houses and on your gates, so that your days and the days of your children may be many in the land that the Lord swore to give your forefathers, as many as the days that the heavens are above the earth" (Deuteronomy 11:18-21).

Do you have a journal where you write down the things that God is doing in your life and the things He is saying to you? Do you make notes in your Bible about verses that become alive to you? Do you record the blessings from God's hand? Listen to what God told His people to do with His words. Pray and ask how you can apply this lesson in your life. It is always good to see how far you have come!

PERFORMANCE PRINCIPLE 71

ILL-GOTTEN GAIN

News out of Lausanne, Switzerland noted that the International Olympic Committee is bracing itself for the onset of a problem more formidable and dangerous than doping—genetic modification of athletes.

Meeting with some of the world's leading genetic experts, representatives of the IOC medal commission examined the potential impact of gene therapy in sports and the ethical implications of genetically modifying athletes.

Major advancements have been made recently in the field of gene therapy, which involves injecting the body with new genes that produce therapeutic proteins meant to block disease. This technique, still in the experimental state, is designed to treat, cure, or prevent disease. But authorities fear some people will try to use gene therapy to secure a competitive edge on the playing field.

Everyone who competes wants to win, but there is only one way to get there—hard work! An athlete who cuts corners, who isn't disciplined, and who doesn't pay the price for victory, will not enjoy the sweet taste that victory in honor brings.

In Proverbs 10:2, King Solomon writes, "Ill-gotten treasures are of no value" (THE MESSAGE). When you have trained and disciplined your body and have endured sacrifice beyond compare, you can step up to the award stand, knowing that the medal being draped around your neck is just reward for your hard work. But if you cheat or cut corners, the medal and all that it represents is meaningless. You may be honored for a day, but the victory will have no meaningful memory for you. In fact, it will leave a bitter taste in your mouth.

Whether you achieve victory or fall short of your dreams, earning your way by integrity and hard work gives a lasting peace and contentment. Its value is more precious than gold, silver, or bronze.

PERFORMANCE PRINCIPLE 72

YOUR CHARACTER IS SHOWING

Sometimes the plan just doesn't work out the way you thought it would. In your mind, you conceived a great season, a year of achievement and high accomplishment. You've planned, you've worked your plan, trained hard, and then somewhere—out of nowhere—disaster strikes. In the blink of an eye an injury pops up unexpectedly. You're dealt a card you don't want in your hand. And all you want to do is cry *why?*

As an athlete, or as a coach, dealing with the unexpected setback is a challenge, especially when it is a season-ending injury. When injuries interfere with dreams, it is gut wrenching. The disappointment is overwhelming. And sometimes you ask yourself why you even put yourself through this pain and turmoil? *Why?*

As warriors on the front line, we expose our hearts and souls in the pursuit of victory and high achievement over and over again. Is there a reason for this heartrending madness?

Air Force head football coach Fisher DeBerry thinks so. "Athletics is a lot like life," says DeBerry. "You can prepare well, but there are setbacks, there are injuries, and there are disappointments. And how you handle those setbacks shows your character."

Character has been defined as the aggregate of features and traits that form the individual nature of some person—the moral or ethical qualities such as integrity. So our character is visible, like a window for others to view who we are and to see what we are made of.

Paul writes in Romans, "We also rejoice in our suffering, because we know that suffering produces perseverance, perseverance produces character, character produces hope, and hope does not disappoint us, because God had poured out his love into our hearts by the Holy Spirit, whom he has given us" (Romans 3:3-5).

You see God has a purpose and a plan in all things (Romans 8:28, Jeremiah 29:11-14). We are to rejoice in our suffering because God uses suffering as a classroom to develop perseverance, character, and hope in us. Without suffering, our development would be incomplete, and we could never be what we could be without it. We would fall short of our full potential.

God's training plan is different than ours (Isaiah 55:8). He has our best interest in mind. So if you want to be in line with God's plan, then rejoice and be glad that He is working His plan in you! How you deal with your suffering, pain, and setback is a window to the world. Show them what you're made of! Show 'em the rock of Christ.

PERFORMANCE PRINCIPLE 73

SEND ME!

When I was a freshman in high school, I joined the wrestling team. I had only a couple of months of experience in junior high school, but I liked the sport. Wrestling was tough and physical, and I thought it would keep me in good shape and help me both in football and baseball, my two favorite sports.

As a freshman I wrestled at 185 pounds. I was a good freshman wrestler, but there was no way that I was varsity material at that time. I didn't know much technique. All I had going for me was strength and a big heart. I would never quit no matter what the score or situation. In practice I would wrestle every day with the sophomore and varsity teams. When we wrestled live in practice, I would battle against the older guys in the same weight class. It wasn't a lot of fun, and I didn't score a lot of points in practice, but it did make me tougher. I like the battle and the challenge, but I hated losing—even in practice.

One day we were scheduled to wrestle against West Chicago High School, one of our conference rivals. West Chicago had a senior 185-pounder named Scott Dierking. Dierking was the returning Illinois State Wrestling Champion and a All-State running back in football. He later went on to be All-Big Ten at Purdue University and played in the backfield for a number of years in the NFL with the New York Jets. Our 185 pound wrestler on varsity wanted no part of Scott Dierking. In fact he told our varsity coach he wouldn't wrestle him.

Like any good wrestling coach, our coach didn't want to

forfeit away six points in a conference dual meet. Coach asked the remaining 185 pound wrestlers on the team, "I need someone to wrestle against Dierking. Who wants to go? We need a full lineup tonight."

"Coach," I said. "I'll go. Send me. I'll wrestle Dierking. I'm not afraid of him. Let me wrestle him!"

Well, I was in the lineup that night. I can clearly remember going to weigh-ins as if it was yesterday. Dierking got on the scale ahead of me—*he was ripped like a Greek god!* His thighs were huge. He was a mass of muscles. Man, it was like David versus Goliath for sure, but I had no rocks or a slingshot to fight with, just my bare hands. I was on my own without a lot of skill, experience, or technique.

I am proud to say, even though I did not win that night, I scored 14 points on the two-time Illinois State champion! Okay, the fact is that Scott took me down 15 times in the first period and let me go 14 times—before he pinned me.

Before the great prophet Isaiah began his ministry he was allowed to see a vision of God seated on the throne in heaven. And he was allowed to witness the full majesty of God. The vision of God was so pure, so holy that Isaiah was immediately confronted with his own sinful condition (Isaiah 6:5).

But God comforted Isaiah by letting him know his sin had been removed. God had a purpose for revealing Himself to Isaiah; He was looking for a messenger to deliver His Word to the people of Israel, "Whom shall I send? And who will go for us?" (Isaiah 6:8).

As a child of God, there can only be one response when our Master Coach calls. There is no need for lengthy questions regarding how, why, or what. When God calls, we need to realize that He knows what He's doing and has made a wise and perfect choice.

God never makes mistakes and will never call us without also providing the tools to accomplish everything in His plan: "God can pour on the blessings in astonishing ways so that you're ready for anything and everything, more than just ready to do what needs to be done" (2 Corinthians 9:8, THE MESSAGE). We have seen His glory and received His forgiveness; now we must trust Him and follow wherever He leads.

When God calls, He always calls the right person for the job, and then provides all we need to fulfill the calling. When God calls, let's trust Him and boldly answer: "Here am I. Send me!"

PERFORMANCE PRINCIPLE 74

SERIOUS PREPARATION

Having been around elite athletes for many years, I am in awe of those who compete in the triathlon. I know what it takes to be the best in one sport; but to excel in swimming, cycling, and running, back-to-back-to-back, blows the most serious of athletes away. My cousin's wife Dolly is a triathlete. What is most exciting about that is that she is closing in on 60 years of age!

Every summer my family heads north to the Upper Peninsula of Michigan to spend a week or two with my cousin's family at their cottage on Big Bay de Noc. While I am out casting my fly rod for smallmouth bass, walking the beach with the dog, or kicking back on the shore with book in hand, Dolly is in serious training.

Before anyone else is up in the morning she is logging in mile after mile on the dusty gravel roads. By mid-morning you can catch her in the garage doing a weight workout with her dumbbells. In the afternoon she'll ask for a ride in my boat. She doesn't want to fish, she just wants to head out about a mile so she can swim back in. In the early evening she jumps on her bike and pedals around the back roads of the Stonington peninsula on her final training segment of the day.

Between all this serious training is shopping, entertaining, preparing meals for huge guest list, and tons of clean-up. Every afternoon you can find her in the hammock at beach's edge in a deep, well needed nap. All of this while on "vacation!"

Preparing for a triathlon is serious business. It requires serious training and serious commitment. There are times in our lives that become serious business. If we are going to overcome the "triathlons" in our lives, we need serious preparation. One method of preparation is fasting.

Even before Christ walked the earth, fasting was a symbol of a person humbling themselves to show God that he or she is sincere in seeking God's blessings. Fasting is serious business. We fast with only one motive and that is *to seek God.*

There are various kinds of fasts:

the absolute fast, which is without water or food and needs to be approached with careful consideration as you are led by the Holy Spirit (Matthew 4:1-3).

the normal fast, which is without food for a limited time – one day up to seven, and sometimes even forty days, but with water or liquids.

the partial fast, which is a limited diet like going without tea, coffee, delectable fare, non-vegetarian, breakfast, or any of the meals during the day for a period of time, (Daniel 10:2).

another type of fast is going without sleep for a night, spending it in prayer. (Luke 6:12)

Fasting always needs to be accompanied by prayer. The essential purpose is to go about your daily routine without making a show of fasting and create additional moments of prayer in our normal schedule of activities. The idea is not to make an issue about personal fasting, whether with lack of food or lack of sleep, but to go about your daily business with a normal attitude, (Matthew 6:17-19).

Such a selfless attitude enables our prayers to be heard and answered as well. God sees the sincerity of our heart, and He is pleased when our motive is simply to do our best to love Him with all our heart, mind, soul, and strength, (Jeremiah 29:12-13).

If you know Jesus Christ as your Master Coach, I encourage you to experience His power through fasting and prayer. I encourage you to fast regularly, not just alone but with like-minded teammates as well. When you commit and train hard, you will begin to see the hand of God move mightily in your own life, in your family's life, in your community, in your school or university, and in your country!

Being a member of God's team is serious business, and it requires serious action. Ready yourself with serious preparation.

Performance Principle 75

Give It Back

A number of years ago when I was living in Florida, I made a trip to Winter Haven with my seven year old son Matt to see my beloved Boston Red Sox in a spring training game against the Detroit Tigers. I recall standing in line for hours just to get a standing-room only ticket. Matt was thrilled to be at his first big league game.

As we stood along the right field foul line, Matt shagged a foul ball. He was so happy to get a major league baseball. His focus now was to get an autograph on his prize.

After the game we stood outside the Red Sox locker room. As the players filed out of the locker room after showering and changing, Matt held the ball in his outstretched arm asking each player that walked by to sign his ball. Not one player signed the ball. In fact, one player whom I held in high esteem, pushed him aside.

On a long ride home I was pretty upset that not one athlete took the time to sign a baseball for the kid. It bothered me that they can sell their signature on a ball, a bat, or on a trading card, but they can't do it for free. The professional game has become "it is all about me." Where was the attitude of old about "giving back to the game"? Is it gone for good?

One day at the temple in Jerusalem, Jesus watched people place their offerings into the temple treasury. He noticed a poor widow who put in two coins valued at less than a penny.

"Jesus called his disciples over and said, 'The truth is that this poor widow gave more to the collection than all the others put together. All the others gave what they'll never miss; she gave extravagantly what she couldn't afford—she gave her all" (Mark 12:43-44 THE MESSAGE).

This passage gives us a wonderful example of faith and how God must be the Lord of our finances—but the message actually goes much deeper than that.

We all have been blessed in a multitude of ways. We are called to be good stewards, or managers, of all our blessings. And as a good steward, we must give everything back to our Heavenly Father as an offering of love. This relates to our financial resources; but it also means we are to offer our gifts, abilities, talents, and time back to God through service and ministry to others. God created us, with every one of our abilities—for a purpose. We will need to spend good quality time with God to determine our purpose, but we can be absolutely sure that God has NOT blessed us so we can advance our own selfish agenda!

Every one of our blessings, no matter how small, is given so we can bless God in return. We often hold back. Sometimes we feel inadequate to serve or we feel even unworthy to make a true contribution to the work of God's Kingdom. It is important to realize that God is not concerned with the gift, but more so with the condition of our heart. "Does the Lord delight in burnt offerings and sacrifices as much as in obeying the voice of the Lord? To obey is better than sacrifice, and to heed is better than the fat of rams," (1 Samuel 15:22). How we give is much more important than what we give.

Recently I was told by a trusted friend that I should draw some pay from "To The Next Level." That I should charge for subscriptions to the site so I can generate funds to publish books, to put on streaming video, to pay for my labors, and to generate funds to advance the ministry. I was told that I give away too much for free.

Man, I just don't see it that way. Coaching is my job, and it pays me a wage and provides for my needs. Sports ministry is my passion. Why? For if it wasn't for sport, for the role models I had as a high school athlete, I might have never found the peace and contentment I was searching for—and I found it all in Jesus.

God has blessed me with talent: He gave me the abilities to coach and motivate young athletes, and He has given me the talent to write, to take a spiritual principle and make it alive through the world of sport. Who should profit from it?

First and foremost, I believe that God should profit from His blessings to me. My number one goal is to bring as many people with me to God's banquet table. So, to give back, I work Fellowship of Christian Athletes summer conference or wrestling camps for free, rather than conducting camps or working camps that will pay me. I do some long term mission trips with Athletes In Action. Most recently I went on a three-week mission trip to Russia to advance the ministry to Muslin athletes in the Caucus Mountain region and to minister to Chechen children who were displaced because of war. To tell you the truth, I got a bigger rush playing Frisbee with Chechen kids and showing them God's love than I ever did coaching any of my past All-Americans.

The sacrifice I lay on God's altar is a love offering—it is giving back from the abundance that He has given me. If we want our service or ministry to have significance in the eyes of God, we first must focus on the One to whom we are giving rather than on the value in the eyes of man.

If God wants me to publish a book, or have streaming video, or even advance the ministry beyond today's scope, I am trusting Him to provide the way.

If our heart is pure in the giving, God will receive our offering as a true blessing. I have one goal—that is to hear from the Master Coach, "Well done good and faithful servant," that is why I am giving it back!

PERFORMANCE PRINCIPLE 76

DO THE RIGHT THING

In the 2003 NCAA I National Wrestling Championships in Kansas City, two collegiate wrestlers battled for All-American honors in the second round of the championship bracket. From the University of Iowa was undefeated Steve Mocco, the top-ranked heavyweight in the nation. From intrastate rival Iowa State was Scott Coleman.

Coleman was being manhandled by Mocco during the match. Mocco attempted to turn Coleman by using a bar-arm and pinning Coleman's head between his knees while working on forcing Coleman to go to his back.

In his excitement and his aggressive style, Mocco elevated the arm of Coleman too high and away from the body. The referee stopped the match and penalized Mocco for an illegal hold. Coleman remained on the mat in pain, barely able to lift his right arm.

According to the rules of wrestling, had Coleman informed the referee he could not continue, the undefeated Mocco would have been disqualified, ending his hope of a national title.

Instead, Iowa State coach Bobby Douglas, who wasn't even initially coaching in his athlete's corner rushed onto the mat and instructed Coleman to return to the mat…for at least one more second…before retiring because of an injury default.

That one second was the difference between a national championship which Mocco eventually earned and a painful dream for Iowa State's Scott Coleman. It also served as a quick reminder to Steve Mocco and many others in Kemper Arena that sportsmanship is measured by more than championships.

According to Coach Douglas, "We did the right thing. It wasn't that he was deliberately trying to hurt him. He got hurt because of the position. If you get in that position and don't go over, you will get hurt."

Life is always going to put you in some tough situations. Our daily actions will reflect our priorities and values. In a sense they are the sacrifices we place on God's altar. Every day we make many decisions which either draw us closer to God or lead us farther away.

Jesus had been found guilty by the Jewish leaders. They commented that, "He is worthy of death!" (Matthew 26:66). But Roman law required a sentence of death to be approved by the Roman Court. Therefore, Jesus was brought before Pontius Pilate, the governor of the region surrounding Jerusalem.

Pilate was in a tough situation. He had talked with Jesus and could find nothing deserving of death, "I have examined Him in your presence and have found no basis for your charges against Him," (Luke 23:14). But Pilate was also under great pressure to keep peace in the region, so he allowed the people of Jerusalem to make the final decision.

"Which one do you want me to release to you: Barabbas, or Jesus who is called the Christ?" (Matthew 27:17)

Barabbas was a convicted murderer—Jesus was the Son of God. The people loved Jesus when He was feeding them or healing their sick, but when required to make a decision, the people chose Barabbas. "What shall I do, then, with Jesus who is called the Christ?' Pilate asked. They all answered, 'Crucify Him!'" (Matthew 27:21-22).

The presence of God is not found through specific prayers or religious activity; rather, the peace of His presence is found through our moment-by-moment choice to allow Jesus to be the Lord of our life, then to follow His leading. We must learn to choose based on what is pleasing to a loving God and not simply on what is "allowable" by the rules!

What part of the crowd are you? Are you one who is easily swayed, or are you willing to stand firm in your faith?

We all face the same decision many times each day as the people in front of Pilate: Jesus or Barabbas? The ways of God or the ways of the world. Life or death? Victory by the rules or sportsmanship?

If we desire a life with God, we must choose wisely. We must boldly face the multitudes of daily decisions and be determined to choose to do the right thing! When we do, we choose Christ.

PERFORMANCE PRINCIPLE 77

ANSWERING THE CALL

There is a time in every athlete's life when the call comes to step up one's game. This is a time of decision, when either you answer or reject the call to take your game to the next level. When the call comes, it is an urge, an inner feeling in one's gut. You can't ignore it for long. Soon it becomes more than a vision—not only can you see, but smell and taste what the future can hold.

The call is an announcement to train harder, to be more disciplined, and to sacrifice. It is a call to tighten up your skills, work on the weakness, and pursue tougher competition. It is a call to commitment, putting aside outside activities and relationships to become the very best you can be. The call always comes with a cost.

I have seen athletes do some radical things when the call came. I have seen athletes become fanatical trainers, when every free moment in their day was used for a running or strength training, or skill development. I have seen athletes avoid fast food, soda pop, and sweets. I have witnessed on more than one occasion athletes ending dating relationships so they could stay focused on their goals.

Responding to the call can bring about some radical changes!

When Jesus began His ministry, He called a few select people to follow Him. There was something special and irresistible about His call—it was a call that opened eyes to a new world order and caused a radical change within.

Jesus said, "If anyone would come after Me, he must deny himself and take up his cross daily and follow Me. For whoever wants to save his life will lose it, but whoever loses his life for Me will save it. What good is it for a man to gain the whole world, and yet lose or forfeit his very self?" (Luke 9:23-25).

Peter, John and James were commercial fisherman on the Sea of Galilee. Everything they owned was tied up in boats, nets, in processing and sales. Fishing was their livelihood and the sole support of their families. Yet when the call from Christ came to become "fishers of men," they dropped their nets, left everything and followed Him, (Luke 5:11).

Matthew, also known as Levi was a Jewish tax collector who worked for the Roman government. Matthew had a good job, made a good wage; but he turned his back on tax collecting and the security which that life provided when Jesus called, "'Follow Me', and Levi got up and left everything and followed Him," (Luke 5:27-28).

There are other examples from the Old Testament as well. Abraham moved his whole family to follow God without knowing where he was being sent (Genesis 12:1-5).

Moses at 80 years old left the peaceful life of tending sheep to follow God's call to confront Pharaoh (Exodus 3).

The bottom line is answering the call will always require a change, but the change does not always mean in location, profession, or status.

There will always be a change when we take up the cross and follow Christ—but the real change comes in our heart. It is a change when we learn "the secret of being content in all circumstances" (Philippians 4:12). There is a change when we "love your neighbor as yourselves" (Matthew 22:38). It is a real change when we leave our old values, priorities, dreams and desires to find fulfillment in following Christ.

As we draw closer to Christ, we will find that His call is irresistible as we see, hear, and taste a little bit more of Heaven every day. No one who has ever answered the call has been disappointed. You will find the sacrifice and the change all worth it!

PERFORMANCE PRINCIPLE 78

PRACTICE PLAN FOR SUCCESS

No person can just read a book and expect to be an athlete. It would be foolish to expect someone to step into the field of competition with book knowledge alone and be successful. Practice in live situations is necessary before anyone should step into the field of battle. It takes thousands upon thousands of perfect repetitions to develop the skills needed to be successful.

Elite coaches spend countless hours in developing periodization plans to peak their athletes at the right time. Everything imaginable is taken into consideration; nutrition, sets and reps in a specific strength program in the weight room, practice volume and intensity, conditioning levels, rest and recovery, acclimatization, travel plans, etc. Practice is becoming an exact science in sport.

Practice schedules today consists of detailed, well thought out plans. Everything that is done in a workout session has a specific purpose to prepare the athlete for a specific situation that is anticipated by the coaching staff. No detail is over looked. A good coach will make sure his athletes are properly prepared for competition both physically, technically, and psychologically.

Paul told his team, the Philippians, this, "Put into practice what you learned from me, what you heard and saw and realized" (Philippians 4:9, THE MESSAGE).

Paul knew and lived God's game plan every day. Paul would have never learned the techniques and secrets of being content of all situations (Philippians 4:12) if he had just learned "about" the gospel. He had to experience it first hand. Even though Paul was a scholar and knew what was written in the scriptures, the real life situations that Paul experienced developed him and prepared him for the bigger trials and tougher battles laid ahead. Paul was properly prepared and was able to be victorious.

Although it is wise to study and learn, the real lessons are learned in the application, the practice of God's Word into the daily battles in our lives.

Today you cannot afford to be just a hearer of God's truths. No, you need to go to practice daily. You need to strap it up and bust it hard in each and every rep. Listen to the Master Coach and do what you are told. Focus and intensity is important.

Hey, you are going to be sore. You'll hurt and you will get knock down a few times. Coach guarantees it. But if the desire is there, if you work hard, study, and get in the game of life and do your best, you will find that Coach has prepared you for victory. Listen, learn and plug into His practice plan for success!

PERFORMANCE PRINCIPLE 79

WHAT DO YOU GOT?

The unique challenge in coaching is taking a group of individuals and molding them into a team. The process is not an easy one. The equation has many variables that need to be calculated carefully.

The coach has to deal with individual strengths and weaknesses, with attitudes, with varying skills, abilities, and talents. A team needs leaders and direction so that they will lead down the right path. The coach will have team members with various levels of commitment, and of course varying levels of work ethic. The successful coach can bring out the best in each of the team members.

The key here is that the coach needs to be attentive to each team member. Too often coaches only look at their starting team, and they only "coach" them. A strategy for coaching success is to know the abilities, strengths, and talents of all the team members, and to make each athlete feel important and needed to the cause.

An attentive coach will know what each athlete can do, what they've got, and when they can do it. Bringing someone off the bench at the right time has won many a ball game.

Every day during Jesus' ministry He was teaching and training His team of followers. As Jesus performed miracles huge crowds began to follow Him. One day Jesus climbed a hill on the Sea of Galilee and was surrounded by thousands of people.

Jesus said to Philip, "Where can we buy bread to feed this

people?" Philip responded, "Two hundred silver pieces wouldn't be enough to buy bread for each person to get a piece." (John 6:7, THE MESSAGE).

One of the other disciples, Andrew said, "There's a little boy here who has five barley loaves and two fish. But that's a drop in the bucket for a crowd like this," (John 6:9, THE MESSAGE).

This little boy was in the most strategic position to assist Christ in teaching a powerful lesson to the disciples, and a great blessing to a multitude of people. There are two lessons here to be learned; first in the hands of Christ, little becomes much! This situation was orchestrated by God to show faith—that even "little" can become very big!

Christ taught and fed thousands of people that day. The 5,000 had seen the miracle that Jesus had performed and said, "This is a Prophet for sure, God's Prophet right here in Galilee!" (John 6).

Lesson two is that because of this boy, 5,000 people realized that Jesus was the Messiah, the Christ! Even though Andrew's view of what the boy had was a "drop in the bucket," Jesus realized what the boy really possessed. Then, He knew how to use it for God glory.

The question is, "What do you got?" What little insignificant drop in the bucket do you possess that God can use? The Master Coach can bless a multitude of people through *you* if you yield yourself and the little that you have. He has a plan, and you are in it! Allow Him to use what you got!

PERFORMANCE PRINCIPLE 80

TOUGH THINGS TO DO

Late greats Ted Williams and Sam Snead, masters of different swings, use to kid each other about whose job was the toughest, hitting a baseball or hitting a golf ball.

Williams often said hitting a baseball was "the hardest thing to do in sports." In a Golf Digest article, he recalled telling Snead that a golf ball is "just sitting there all pretty, snow white, smiling, teed up, everybody's quiet like a church," while a baseball hitter faces fastballs and curves from all angles with fans screaming.

"Yeah, I know," said Slammin' Sammy Snead, "but when we hit a foul ball, we got to go out and play it."

Both had a point. The topic is one that fans have debated for a long time: What is the hardest thing to do in all of sports?

A USA Today poll ranked it this way:

Hitting a baseball
Race car driving
Pole vaulting
Hitting a long, straight tee shot in golf
Returning a tennis serve
Landing a quadruple jump in figure skating
Running a marathon (26.4 miles)
Competing in the Tour de France bike race
Saving a penalty kick in soccer
Down hill ski racing

I guess we could all argue about the poll… how about the Ironman Triathlon? Or dropping to your knees to stop a 105 mph slap shot, or luging at over 90 mph down a track made of ice, or sticking a landing after going off a ski jump, or taking head and body blows from a heavyweight boxer? There is a lot to consider in what is the toughest thing to do in sport.

Over the ages many people have been determined to do the toughest thing of all—saving themselves. They have tried to open the gates of eternal salvation by being a good person, by doing good works (donating money, helping the poor, volunteering time, etc.), or by following the rules and regulations of religion.

The bottom line is—you can't save yourself. It is impossible! The Bible tells us that, "The wages of sin is death," (Romans 6:23). Man is inherently sinful—in fact, we don't have a chance without a savior. The Old Testament prophet Isaiah writes, "all our righteous acts are like filthy rags," (Isaiah 64:6).

There is only one way to heaven, and it goes through Jesus Christ. Jesus said, "I am the way, the truth, and the life. No one goes to the Father except by me." (John 14:6).

One of the toughest things to do in life is to realize is the fact that you indeed need a Savior—then to surrender to Him. We are taught in sport to never surrender, to fight until the end, to never quit. The lessons of the world do get in the way. Pride gets in the way, money gets in the way, and friends and family can get in the way too.

Yet, one of the easiest things to do is to ask Jesus to come into your life. Jesus is patiently waiting to hear from you. It can be as simple as bowing your head right now and asking Him to come into your heart. Don't wait a moment longer to start your new life in Jesus Christ. Pray this prayer:

"Father, I know that I have broken your laws and my sins have separated me from you. I am truly sorry, and now I want to turn away from my past sinful life toward you. Please for-

give me, and help me avoid sinning again. I believe that your son, Jesus Christ died for my sins, was resurrected from the dead, is alive, and hears my prayer. I invite Jesus to become the Lord of my life, to rule and reign in my heart from this day forward. Please send your Holy Spirit to help me obey You, and to do Your will for the rest of my life. In Jesus' name I pray, Amen."

If you've prayed this prayer of salvation with true conviction and heart, you are now a Christian—a member of God's Team! This is a fact, whether or not you feel any different. Religious systems may have led you to believe that you should feel something—a warm glow, a tingle, or some other mystical experience. The fact is, you may, or you may not. The Bible tells us that your eternal salvation is secure! "That if you confess with your mouth, "Jesus is Lord," and believe in your heart that God raised him from the dead, you will be saved" (Romans 10:9).

Welcome to God's team! I encourage you now to find a local church where you can be baptized and grow in the knowledge of God through His Word, the Bible.

Truthfully, the toughest thing is to endure life without Him. That's one thing you don't want to do!

WWW.TOTHENEXTLEVEL.ORG

TO THE NEXT LEVEL, directed by Coach Doug Reese, is your on-line coach providing practical training tips, nutritional advice, strength and conditioning suggestions, mental skills training, counseling and motivational techniques. If you have a sports specific question—ask our panel of pro, collegiate, and Olympic coaches in "Ask the Coach."

For the coach/trainer, TTNL provides a clinic-like opportunity at your fingertips—"Coaching Development" and "Program Development" sections provides sound advice to take your coaching and your sport program to the next level. Our "Coaches Forum" brings coaches from around the world together in a one-on-one coaching clinic.

To The Next Level is a Christ-centered ministry dedicated to educate, inspire, and motivate athletes and coaches, and all whom they influence to achieve their full human, spiritual, and athletic potential in reaching the next level through a life changing relationship with Jesus Christ.

If you are serious about your sport—log on to TTNL, where our goal is to help you bring life and sport to the next level.

With over a quarter of a million hits per month on our website, we are reaching over 70 countries with the message of how you can reach your full potential as an athlete or coach—both on and of the field. We welcome your visit.

About the AUTHOR

Doug Reese is originally from Geneva, IL where he was an outstanding three-sport athlete. As a sophomore in high school Reese made a personal commitment to Christ at a Billy Graham Crusade. Since that time, Reese has been a very active participant in the sport ministries of the Fellowship of Christian Athletes and in Athletes In Action.

Reese is a graduate of Northern Michigan University. Following graduation, Reese was hired at Wheaton North High School (IL) where he coached the offensive line in football and was head girl's softball coach. The very next season Reese joined the football coaching staff at Wheaton College (IL) for one year, then took a position as offensive line coach at Michigan Technological University for four seasons.

For four years Reese served as assistant head football coach and head wrestling coach at Hernando High School in Brooksville, Florida where he was named both *Gulf Coast Conference* and *Tampa Tribune* Coach of the Year.

Reese then joined the athletic department at the University of Minnesota-Morris as head wrestling coach and as assistant to the Athletic Director. During his tenure at UM-Morris Reese has coached men's collegiate wrestling, women's freestyle wrestling, football, and women's cross country.

In twelve seasons at UM-Morris, Reese has developed 122 All-Americans, 33 Academic All-Americans, and has produced 16 U.S. National Team Members, with 11 of his athletes representing the United States in world championship competition.

Reese has achieved recognition as a *Gold Level Certified Coach* from USA Wrestling, and has coached in five world championships and the Pan-American Championships.

Coach Reese is very active in the Fellowship of Christian Athletes, serving most recently as a summer conference speaker and clinician, and he is also a strong supporter of Athletes In Action, participating in missions trips to Central America and to Russia with AIA Wrestling.